A BLUEPRINT TO LIVING YOUR BEST LIFE

Unleash Your SHERO

A COMPILATION BY WOMEN CONQUERING TO WIN!

ERICA PERRY GREEN

UNLEASH YOUR SHERO:

A BLUEPRINT TO LIVING YOUR BEST LIFE

Copyright ©2017 Erica Perry Green

Scripture quotations are taken from the Holy Bible, New Living Translation, copyright © 1996, 2004, 2007, 2013, 2015 by Tyndale House Foundation. All rights reserved.

PUBLISHING

Published by: SHERO Publishing & Smart Choice Publishing

SHERO Publishing
340 S. Lemon Ave #9608, Walnut, CA 91789
Info@sheromagazine.com
ericaperrygreen.com/shero-publishing

Cover Design & Layout by SHERO Publishing
Editing: SynergyEd Consulting
Photography: Synergy Photography ~ Kimberly Perry-Sanderlin

Printed by: Impress Print & Graphics ~ P.O. Box 13794 RTP, NC 27709
Printed in the United States of America
Library of Congress Cataloging-in-Publication Data

ISBN-10: 0-9994470-0-9
ISBN-13: 978-0-9994470-0-0

For copies, event bookings & trainings, author requests and publishing information, call 803-757-4376

I prayed that God would cover this compilation project and send the right women to bless everyone who would read the pages of this book. God sent 13 extraordinary women to join me in sharing their testimonies with the world.

To each of these ladies, I say, *THANK YOU* for entrusting me with your words and for sharing them in this literary work.

Erica Perry Green

SHERO
PUBLISHING

Dedication

This book is dedicated to every woman, around the world, who will read the testimonies and apply the strategies to overcome the obstacles that impede her greatness.

May the words shared help you to *Unleash Your Shero!*

-God Bless,
Erica Perry Green

Acknowledgments

Firstly, giving honor to my Lord and Savior, Jesus Christ, whom without, I wouldn't be here today. As I look back over my life, I marvel at how God has kept me here to share my testimonies and walk in HIS purpose for me. All I can say is, "Thank you Lord."

To my husband, my partner in crime and my biggest supporter, Jonathan Green, thank you for encouraging me to keep going and pushing me to share this project with the world.

To my beautiful, intelligent, and very artistic daughter, Camryn Nicole Green, I thank you for always cheering me on and pushing me to be the very best role model that I can for you. I strive to make you proud daily. Always know that everything I do, is for you. I love you dearly.

To my amazing family who are my supporters and consultants; my father, Euric LaBruce Perry, my mother, Linda Simons Perry and sister, Kimberly Perry-Sanderlin, there are no words to thank you for your support throughout this project and in every aspect of my life. Thank you for always cheering me on.

To my amazing nephew, Chauncey Sanderlin- You make your auntie work hard daily. Your belief that Aunt E can do anything, pushes me to fulfill the greatness that you see in me. Know that Aunt E loves you and will always have your back.

To my spiritual mothers, Pastor Tilda Whitaker, Apostle Cassandra Sampson and Minister Helen Lawrence, thank you for always covering what God has put in me to give to the world. To my amazing friend and dear sister, Sharonette Smart, thank you for your mentorship and support throughout this project.

To the women of Sisters Lifting Sisters Nonprofit and the followers of SHERO Magazine, thank you for your collaboration to give and support Women At Risk.

I pray that this book blesses you all.

Contents

DEDICATION   4

ACKNOWLEDGMENTS   5

ERICA PERRY GREEN   7

SHAWANDA JONES   23

DEBBIE FOREMAN   35

NATASHA PERRY   47

KIMBERLY PERRY SANDERLIN   59

TYEASIA KIAH   71

JASMINE CORDELL ARMSTRONG   81

TILDA WHITAKER   95

HELEN LAWRENCE   107

KIM WILSON   125

SHARONETTE SMART   137

SHERESA ELLIOT   149

CHEMEKA TURNER-WILLIAMS   157

LAKESHA LAKES   171

Author Erica Perry Green

Erica Perry Green is truly a woman who has risen from **TRIALS 2 TRIUMPH!** An accomplished healthcare professional and business leader, Erica has an innate passion for helping others. She has focused her career on doing just that. As a graduate of The University of North Carolina's School of Public Health, Erica has worked in Corporate America, for over a decade, in Pharmaceutical Sales, Physician Training, Healthcare Sales & Marketing and currently as a Regional Healthcare Sales Manager; all careers that place her directly in a coaching and consulting capacity.

While rising through the ranks in Corporate America, Erica had a strong desire to own her own business and create a legacy that would out-live her. For over 6 years, Erica has been successful in various business endeavors, ascended to top ranks in two global businesses and created a network of thousands of business partners. As a skilled entrepreneur, Erica has traveled the world, training and assisting new business owners in growing and developing their brand. Erica is passionate about mentoring and developing successful entrepreneurs and educating others on multiple streams of income.

Erica is a master at turning tragedy into triumph! After facing two tragic, near-death experiences, she recovered with grace, elegance and a powerful conviction that anything can be accomplished with GOD. Erica strives to share her life experiences, in an effort to empower other women. As founder of **Trials 2 Triumph Coaching**, Erica is utilizing her 15+ years of professional and entrepreneurial experience to bless other women seeking to find their purpose, establish a nonprofit, strategically establish and market a business or rise in their professional career.

With an intense passion for giving back, Erica founded **SISTERS LIFTING SISTERS**, a nonprofit that serves and supports **WOMAN AT RISK.** SLS is focused on empowering women and children by bridging the gap between those who need assistance and available local resources. SLS is also a collaborative support network, bringing over 25 women and youth groups, organizations and nonprofits together to produce collaborative events and community service efforts.

To date, SLS has reached over 5,300 women, across numerous countries. SLS supports three Triangle shelters for homeless women and women fighting domestic violence and substance abuse. SLS also supports women at risk by sponsoring an emergency food & clothing pantry for single moms and by raising funds to provide gifts for over 1,500 shelter women and children, over the last six Christmas holidays. Erica is a strong believer of **GIVING BACK**, therefore, every SLS event gives back to support the needs of women within the community that they are serving. Erica wants all women to know that they are not alone and they too, can **RISE AGAINST ALL ODDS**!

In 2016, Erica launched **SHERO MAGAZINE**, highlighting those women who are giving back in their communities. SHERO salutes those silent community warriors who often go unrecognized. In 2017, Erica launched **SHERO PUBLISHING,** to assist women in becoming authors. As an author in the anthology, *Wake. Pray. Slay,* Erica knows the power of sharing your testimony and desires to help other women do the same. *Unleash Your Shero* is the first anthology in this empowerment series.

Throughout all of her philanthropic endeavors, family remains first! Erica enjoys traveling and spending time with her loving husband and business partner, Jonathan Green, and daughter, Camryn.

Get To Know Author Erica Green:

For information on Speaking & Coaching Packages: EricaPerryGreen.com
Nonprofit: SistersLiftingSisters.org

Unleash Your SHERO, for publishing information, visit:
SHEROPublishing.com. To share your community service work or advertise your business, visit: SHEROMagazine.com

Erica Perry Green

Unleashing Destiny

Ever wonder if there was more to life? If there was more that you should be doing? It never fails. At some point, these questions sneak up on you like a thief in the night, robbing you of your ability to be comfortable in your complacency. For me, the questions of a purpose unfulfilled started to show their face before my 30th birthday.

I have always stuck to the plan. Go to school. Get good grades. Stay out of trouble. Graduate. Go to college. Graduate in four years. Find a good job. That was the plan and that was exactly what I did. I grew up knowing these expectations, in my house were without exception. There were some things that I did not have a choice on and excellence in my education was one of those.

My father was a principal and my mother was an educational consultant and instructional supervisor; thus, education was a theme in the Perry household. My parents are both brilliant individuals with multiple degrees and achieved honors in their profession. They forged leadership pathways throughout Northeastern rural, North Carolina. They were pillars of our community and we, as their children, were raised to live up to the example that they provided for us.

Having parents that were educators was not easy! My father was an elementary school principal in our county. Growing up in a small rural farming town, in Northeastern, North Carolina, doctors, lawyers, principals and teachers were some of the most prestigious professions. Everyone in town knew my father. No matter where we went, someone would stop us and say, "Hey Mr. Perry" or "Remember me, Mr. Perry?" Sometimes this notoriety was welcomed and sometimes it was a burden; mainly with my friends. You see, many of my childhood friends and middle school classmates had my father as their principal.

Many of whom were afraid to even set foot in my house! I can remember my friends joking about having Mr. Perry walk the halls, reprimanding students, or even share a time or two that they personally felt the pain of his wooden paddle for doing some mischievous thing that got them sent to the Principal's office. This always made me feel as though I had to set an example for everyone. I had to prove to my teachers and friends that I was the stellar daughter of these highly successful educators. I also had to make my parents proud. I tried hard to avoid doing anything at school that would embarrass them or tarnish the Perry family legacy; well I tried!

Don't get me wrong, I got in my share of trouble and even found my rear end meeting the wooden paddle a time or two, but for the most part, I tried to steer clear from the drama.

So, true to form, I did exactly what was laid out in my plan. I graduated from high school and was accepted into the only school to which I had applied; the only school that I deemed as an appropriate match for me- The University of North Carolina at

Chapel Hill. I still remember the day that I stepped onto the campus; it was as if God had reached down and placed me in a special place, my special place, I was home!

I hit the campus of UNC ready to go conquer the world and was quickly hit with the realities of the elevated standards of a world-renown university. Within days of stepping onto the campus, I realized that the 4-year clock had started to tick and while I learned to navigate the campus of over 30,000, I was faced with the fact that everyone was the best of the best and my good was no longer good enough. This was the first time in my life that I was overwhelmingly challenged. The courses were harder than I had ever faced and my freshmen counterparts came from states and areas with more advantages than I had experienced.

For the first few weeks this shook me to my core. I asked myself if I was good enough; if I was worthy of being here? As I watched my roommate fail to keep her grades afloat, the harsh reality of what could become my situation literally slapped me in the face. I knew that I would have to dig deep to make this work.

Looking back, I now know that this was the first time that God started to reveal my purpose and gifted power.

I knew that I would need assistance to make it at UNC, so I decided to schedule appointments with every professor on my very long semester schedule. While most of my friends were avoiding our professors' scheduled office hours like the plague, I decided to use them to my advantage. I met with the professors and shared my current situation and my vision for my future. I quickly realized that conversations, initiated by my desperation to pass my courses, turned into unbelievable opportunities to excel in ways unimaginable. As I sat with professors, they began to give me recommendations on books to read, pages to study, next courses to take. The professors had tons of free time, as I was usually the only one who showed up. As I shared my visions with them, they all seemed eager to help elevate me to the next level. Some even gave me recommendations and referrals for The School of Public Health.

During these discussions, I learned that I had a gift to sell a vision and create buy-in from others. I was able to walk into a room and get those around me to want to be a part of my vision. The more that I painted the picture, the more that the professors freely gave to assist me. I realized that I was a natural-born seller. While I never thought of going into sales as a career, it is amazing how God can align you with your purpose.

Throughout college, I found myself in leadership positions. I was always the one volunteering to lead the group or speak on behalf of my Health Policy Team. I was the one picked as the nursing station lead on the labor and delivery floor at UNC Hospital, and the sales lead at Hudson Belk Department Store. I was called upon to assume leadership roles throughout my college organizations and community outreach. My ability to sell myself helped me to gain acceptance to UNC's prestigious School of Public Health, and ultimately earn a Health Policy and Administration degree. I graduated with two main career routes; hospital consulting or pharmaceutical sales. I chose the later.

As I moved into my career in pharmaceutical sales, my innate sales skills started to re-emerge and my sales success soared. I had no problem gaining the trust and respect of physicians and hospital staff. I also realized that I was a natural-born problem-solver who enjoyed the challenge of looking at what is not working in a situation and making it better. While my career allowed me to utilize these skills and improve the quality of lives for patients throughout my state, I still felt a pulling to do more.

Sometimes we feel the pull on our lives and we resist. It is so easy to go to work and come home and flip on the TV; zoning out the rest of the world. Many of us do this day in and day out, but we go through life with this emptiness or unfulfilled yearning. I hear this all the time in my coaching of clients. Many know that there is more for them to do, they just need to find it.

For me, I started to discover my path to destiny six years into my professional career. While I continued to have great success in Corporate America, I had this desire to help others and to serve. I started mentoring colleagues at work. While others were unwilling to share their techniques for success, I enjoyed helping colleagues reach new levels of professional success. I was quickly plucked out for my company's management development program and began the process of becoming a manager and coach. While I loved the rush of achieving personal sales success, I found greater joy in supporting my team's success and growth.

I began to look outside of my profession for other ways that I could serve and give. I was conflicted by the need for balance between work and personal life and often questioned whether I had the time or energy to do more. Even with this apprehension, I continued to feel the pull that there was more for me to do. It was as if I could hear God saying, *"You still have work to do my child."* These words have echoed in my mind numerous times throughout my life. As I faced many storms, I always heard God's voice calling me to keep going, to keep pressing on. Even when I tried to ignore this burning in my belly, it always came bubbling to the surface like an erupting volcano. I couldn't contain it.

I knew that I wanted to do something in the community, so I sought out nonprofit mentors and began the process of developing my own nonprofit. As I have always been passionate about women's issues, I knew that this was the group that I wanted to serve. In 2014, I founded *Sisters Lifting Sisters*, a nonprofit for Women in Crisis. This allowed me to serve single mothers, women fighting health issues and women battling homelessness. I began to partner with shelters and rehabilitation centers.

As I worked with women who faced domestic violence, drug abuse and the battles of being a single mother or women who simply wanted to find their purpose or become a business owner, I started to feel a drive and purpose like never before! While the toy drives, empowerment workshops, seminars and coaching sessions consumed my nights and weekends, I had this new life and new energy and excitement! You see, when you are walking in your purpose and destiny, the work is effortless. God gifts you the energy to serve; the energy to give. I was driven by something bigger than me and my new vigor spilled into every aspect of my life.

You always gain more than your sacrifice. I found that to definitely be true for me. The more that I gave, the more joy and purpose entered my life. I could see the world and life differently and I started to understand why I was here. It never failed; God would draw women to me who had been through obstacles similar to those that I had experienced. I was able to share my testimony and inspire them. Everything that I had been through, God was using it all to bless and empower others.

In and effort to continue to serve and empower women, I founded the *SHERO Empowerment LLC;* including *SHERO Business & Marketing Coaching Services, SHERO Magazine* and *SHERO Publishing Company;* all focused on empowering and developing women to *Unleash Their SHERO Within.*

There is a difference between complacency and destiny. Once I decided to move past my fears and allow God to lead my life, I walked right into what He had destined for me. I now serve and give in a way that fills me with great joy and completeness. I have an internal excitement for life and an absolute need to serve. Never let the demands of others rob you from reaching your destiny. It is yours and yours alone to achieve!

What I Have Learned: Wisdom From a SHERO

- **Response determines your destiny-** It's not the bad things that happen to us, but how we respond to them. It took me a long time to realize that the horrible things that happened were not punishing me; they were *shaping* me. There are things that happen to you that will either defeat you or elevate you to destiny. It is up to you to determine how they shape your life. When I lost my daughter or was faced with the grim diagnosis of needing open-heart surgery, I had to make the choice on how to respond. My response was clear; *what doesn't kill me, makes me stronger.* You see, I understand that we go through some things in life, not just for us, but for others. There is a testimony in every test and while you will never see it while you are in the midst of that storm, you must have faith that it is there. The way you see your life will determine it. Your perspective on things is critical; your response is everything!

- **Never leave your destiny in the hands of others-** Sometimes we allow life and others to guide our paths without taking the reins and steering our own ship. We all have the ability to set goals and take control of our destiny. Yes, we have the demands of our jobs to fulfill, but ask yourself, "What is it that really makes me feel alive? Where do I thrive?" Take time to carve out what sparks that passion inside of you and move towards it. Set measurable goals to attain your dreams and work towards them daily. While I strongly believe in seeking the advice and guidance of coaches and mentors; as they are vital to your goal attainment and advancement towards your destiny, it is also important to find your quiet place. In order to truly hear what God has for you and the direction that He desires for you to go, you must learn to shut out all the noise of life and find your quiet place. Whether you have a prayer room, a solitary chair or just take time to go into a bathroom and shut the door, it is imperative that you learn to close the door on the world and allow God to truly work in your life. It is so easy to go through your day without really giving God and open door. There are so many things pulling at us daily and it can seem that night falls in the blink of an eye. Schedule time for God. Whether it is turning off the radio and meditating in your car or closing your door for 15 minutes of "quiet time" when you get home, this time is essential to keep you centered and focused on aligning your destiny and purpose walk.

- **Seek Your Service-** We are all here to serve humanity in some way. The question is, what is your service? The challenge of life is to find out how you will use your gifts to serve others. I always knew that I wanted to help people, so seeking a career in healthcare and later developing a nonprofit, were just natural ways to position me to serve. Our lives are bigger than ourselves. We all fit into the puzzle of the world and there is something that God planted specifically in you, to bless, heal, restore and support others. Our task is to determine what that is and follow it. Whether you are a hairdresser and your gift is to restore confidence in those suffering from hair loss or you are a teacher unlocking the potential of a young mind or a social worker, protecting those who can not speak for themselves, you are destined to serve others. Every day, we have gifts to give to the world. Your job is to determine who you are destined to serve and how. Once you achieve that, your path to your destiny will follow.

- **You have to have a plan to achieve your destiny-** Nothing great is accomplished without a plan! Destiny and greatness takes planning and execution. Once you know what you desire to do, you must research it, gain insight from the experts and create a solid plan. I rely on vision boards and business plans. I have a daily plan for executing tasks. When you take on more, you have to be more organized and efficient to get it all done. Yes, it is possible, but you must execute with excellence to reach your destiny. Create your plan to walk in your purpose!

- **There is a deeper JOY in finding your destiny-** When you start to walk in your destiny, you will find yourself living on purpose. You will feel a deeper fulfillment in life and a greater joy. Understanding your purpose opens your eyes to the true power of your existence; the true power of your life!

You Have The Power To Unleash Your SHERO

Author Shawanda Jones

Shawanda Jones, often called "Mz Shay" is a U.S. Navy veteran currently residing in Augusta, Georgia. Born an only child, Shawanda was raised in San Antonio, Texas. Shawanda honorably served in the military for eight years. As a Petty Officer Second Class, Shawanda was stationed in Parris Island, SC and Pearl Harbor, Hawaii.

After ending her military career, Shawanda continued to strive for excellence by returning to school to further her education, where she graduated Magna Cum Laude with her Bachelor's degree in Criminal Justice from Everest University. Currently, Shawanda is working to obtain a Masters of Healthcare Administration. Although she is now a veteran, Shawanda continues to work within the military environment; working and serving injured active duty Army, Army Reserve and National Guard soldiers who undergo medical evaluation boards at Fort Gordon, Georgia.

In 2000, Shawanda married her best friend, Russell Jones, Jr and they were blessed with two beautiful children, Trinity Jones and Nehemiah Gilmore-Jones.

As a two-time author, Mz Shay's published novels are entitled: *Just Love Me: De'Asia's Journey* and *Just Love Me: De'Asia's Journey 2*. When she is not giving back to her fellow military comrades, Shawanda enjoys writing novels and spending quality time with her beautiful family.

Shawanda Jones
Unleashing The Angry Black Woman

Leaving a rough neighborhood in San Antonio, Texas and enlisting in the United States Navy was the beginning of my struggle. An only child who was surrounded by violence, I boldly transitioned into the structured environment. While I was navigating uncharted territories, my parents separated and broke my heart. To say the world as I knew it was shattered, is an understatement. None of this made any sense to me; there were no prior indications of my parents separating. From birth until I graduated high school and joined the Navy, my parents together was the only constant in my life. Living twelve hundred miles away from home, which was my comfort zone, interrupted my inner peace. Unable to make sense of this separation tore my world apart and caused me to rebel. Pent-up frustrations caused me to fight other females, disrespect authority, and develop a reckless attitude.

During my period of internal warfare, I met my future husband, a Marine who would significantly impact my life. We were both stationed at Parris Island, South Carolina and the attraction was instant. After two years of dating my future husband, I was discharged from the Navy. Having to transition from using my fists to using my words was close to impossible. Consequently, I was honorably discharged after my first four-year contract was completed. No one took the time to figure out why my instincts were to fight without ever thinking twice. No one understood or seemed to care about the hood girl with the quick temper and horrible tongue that cut like a samurai sword. I never went to a therapist, but was labeled as having a personality disorder. To ever re-enter the Navy, a psychiatric waiver would be required. This left a dejected twenty-two-year-old displaced from the military, without a plan for her future.

My only conceivable option was relocating back to Texas. Thus began a long-distance relationship with my boyfriend. Six months later, he was discharged and I relocated to Florida so that we could move in together. Unbeknownst to me, his immediate family had an issue with him dating an African American. I struggled with trying to understand why Native Americans, who are a minority as well, would have an issue with us being together. Naively trying to build a relationship with his family caused many arguments.

We were married roughly two years after moving in together. My family drove from Texas to attend the wedding. Unfortunately, the majority of his family, who resided locally, declined our wedding invitation. Our first child, a daughter, was born two years after we were married. I prayed the birth would be the new beginning we needed to forge some sort of extended "family." No such luck.

Imagine being with your significant other; running into one of their family members at a grocery store and not being acknowledged. A full conversation transpires and it's as though you are not even present. Imagine reading a letter from a close family member and discovering they felt "God didn't intend for races to mix." I can't explain the feeling I had, reading those words about me!

We received a few unannounced visits; my husband's relatives walked into our home and not so much as uttered two syllables to me. My response was typical; I aggressively struck back with what I was used to. I did everything from blocking them from calling my home to cursing one of them out! I would get so angry that I wanted to fight! I didn't deserve the treatment I received and had never seen ignorance like this before in my life.

Of course, in their eyes, I was the evil one. I was the one who had the problem. It's amazing how the actions of others appear perfectly fine to them. The moment you push back is when the problem arises. Never one to back down from a fight of any kind, I internalized the tensions and became the one who had so much hatred in my heart. Just the mention of their names instantly put me on the defense. It gradually got to the point that I did not require a reason to ignite on my husband's family. They didn't have to mistreat me or act as though I was of lesser class. I went from zero to one hundred immediately, when anything relating to them occurred. I had become the stereotypical "Angry, Black Woman."

It was as if I could only articulate my thoughts and feelings through violence and profanity.

Obviously, all of this began to seep into my marriage. It wasn't long before I began to resent my husband and felt he wasn't properly putting his relatives in their place. Maybe I couldn't see past the anger. It felt as though I didn't have anyone on my side. Not only was there a battle with my relatives; now my husband and I were at odds as well. Once I realized his family would never accept me, it was pointless to continue to live so far away from home. After dealing with the ignorance for a several years, I decided to move back home to Texas. The distance didn't lessen the hatred I felt in my heart for my husband's family. However, life was now bearable, not having to deal with the drama up close and personal.

The first year of returning home was rough. To make ends meet, my husband and I worked for several temp agencies. Once we had steady income, we focused on having another baby. Several miscarriages and two failed in-vitro fertilization procedures sent me into deep depression. I couldn't understand why God didn't love me enough. In my mind, He allowed my heart to break after each miscarriage and unsuccessful fertility treatment. My husband couldn't bear the emotional rollercoaster and decided we were done trying for another baby. Once my dream was shattered, I decided to focus on returning to the military. Although we had finally secured decent jobs, I didn't feel as though I was living up to my full potential. After months of psychological evaluations and written statements, I was given another opportunity to provide a better life for my daughter!

Being stationed at Pearl Harbor was both exciting and disappointing. I was fast tracked and made rank rather quickly. This was the first time I was ever in a supervisory role and without a doubt, I was determined to make a career out of my second chance. My first assignment was on a ship; more time was spent out to sea than in port. During my tour, I had health issues that required surgery. Having surgery shortened a normal tour of three years down to two years. Post-surgery, complication after complication prevented me from properly healing and returning to finish my ship tour. Consequently, I was referred to a medical board for determination of my fitness to continue serving in the Navy. The pressure of disappointing my family weighed heavily on my heart.

As my career hung in the balance, God blessed me and I got pregnant. After numerous heartbreaking miscarriages and fertility misfortunes, I was finally having another baby! Three months later, my medical board findings were back. It was determined that I was fit to stay in the Navy. However, I wasn't medically fit for ship duty. God had orchestrated my situation to keep me off the ship!

Life was finally looking up for me. I was now stationed and able to focus on bringing a healthy baby into this world. Everything was going perfectly until four months from delivery of my baby, when I discovered the Administration Chief had requested for my naval career to end after my contract was completed. Blindsided, I unsuccessfully filed every complaint imaginable. Within six months, a mother of two would watch yet another dream become a nightmare.

While this was a crushing blow, I was determined not to give up. I filed every appeal possible. I refused to let the military take my dream from me, without having a voice! Life had finally gone the way I planned; how could this happen to me again? I couldn't understand why this was happening to me until the words of my daughter made everything plain.

"Mommy, you owe me an apology," my seven-year old said sternly. Perplexed, I asked her - "why"? My daughter replied, "For going back to the Navy." Her words were heart wrenching. Here I thought I was giving her what she needed; a decent bank account and a nicer home than we ever had, but my daughter wanted her mommy home with her every night. I cried harder than I ever had in my life. Irreplaceable special occasions were taken from us, while I was serving. I missed Mother's Days, birthdays, wedding anniversaries, and Thanksgivings.

Life is funny; I was fighting to be where I wasn't wanted. Meanwhile, my daughter was fighting to make me see where I was needed. Once we ended our military chapter, Georgia became our home. I was determined to pursue my college degree and within just two years, I graduated Magna Cum Laude with a Bachelor's degree in Criminal Justice. Then, God blessed me with a secure job in the Department of Defense.

For five years, I have assisted Army soldiers who are undergoing medical boards. In October, my husband and I will celebrate seventeen years of marriage. Our fifteen-year-old daughter is excelling at her magnet school and our rambunctious miracle baby boy is entering first grade. Within six months, I published my first two novels and have now finished my first collaborative anthology piece. It wasn't until I allowed God to direct my path that I began to receive blessing upon blessing. I am far from perfect, however, I serve an awesome God who guides and walks beside me.

What I Have Learned: Wisdom From A SHERO

- **A Heart of Discernment-** Before I could effectively focus on overcoming any obstacle, it was imperative to seek guidance from God. I prayed for wisdom in determining good from evil. None of my previous decisions were of God; I impulsively reacted in the moment. To receive blessings, letting go of hatred and a cleansed heart were crucial. I'm a work in progress; there are instances when I fall short. Nevertheless, I am a woman of God, who continues to pray for wisdom in making Godly decisions.

- **Gain Perspective and Control-** Decipher whether the problem/situation you're undergoing is a disaster or simply just an inconvenience. Dealing with mental illness sometimes causes small difficulties to appear catastrophic. Making a list of items out of my control helps tremendously. Whatever is placed on this list is no longer my focal point. My attention is primarily on what I can control: my actions, decisions, and thoughts.

- **Count Your Blessings Not Your Problems-** Although it's inevitable to experience trials and tribulations, your blessings will always outweigh the strife in your life. On those dark days, I think of all the blessings God has bestowed upon me. The love of my husband and kids allows small problems to appear insignificant. When you measure the wrong against the things going right in your life; all the problems seem trivial.

- **Avoid Toxic People-** Amid difficulties and misfortunes, the judgment of negative people can drain your energy. Avoid critical, unreliable, and unsupportive people. It's important to surround yourself with positive people who genuinely love and care about you. Oftentimes, simple words of encouragement can minimize the pain or distress you are encountering. Ensure your "supporters" aren't spectators who are anticipating your downfall. The company you keep can potentially cause more damage than the difficulty you are experiencing.

- **Perfectly Imperfect-** There will be days when the walls will seem as though they are closing in on me. There will be days when it appears everyone around me is dancing, as the warm feel of shining sun caresses their skin. Meanwhile, I will run and seek shelter since all I will see and feel are dark clouds and icy raindrops. I may cry out of frustration, whereas, someone else may have the capability of discussing their feelings. Understanding everyone feels and heals differently is my solace.

My goal is constant growth to transform into the best me I can be. There are times when I fall short. Nevertheless, I refuse to give up and will continue to push forward. When life gets tough, I'm encouraged by my progression as opposed to where I used to be.

Psalm 27: 1-3 The LORD is my light and my salvation whom shall I fear? The LORD is the stronghold of my life – of whom shall I be afraid? When the wicked advance against me to devour me, it is my enemies and my foes who will stumble and fall. Though an army besiege me, my heart will not fear, though war break out against me, even then I will be confident.

Author Debbie Foreman

In business as in life, Debbie had humble beginnings and though she was born with a burning desire to succeed, she had yet to find the vehicle to take her to the heights she was destined to aspire. But even in the midst of that life, Debbie had a dream. Inside she knew she would rise above it all. She was determined never to be a product of her environment. Her upbringing taught her strength, resilience and fight. Debbie had a strong desire to empower women to want more out of life.

Debbie works as a Processing Assistant for the NC Nutrition Services Branch. She resides with her amazing husband and twin girls in Nashville, NC. Her twins are currently Juniors in college.

She is a Wife, Mother, Entrepreneur and Author who has an unwavering desire and dedication to *Level Women Up to Their True Worth*.

Get to know Author Debbie Foreman:

www.instagram.com/sparkyourpassion2017

www.sparkyourpassion.weebly.com

Debbie Foreman

Unleashing Bondage

This voyage begins for me with my move from New Jersey to Chesapeake, VA. I was just starting high school and was what they called a nerd. Ninth grade was an awkward year. This was the year of possibilities, forging new friendships and having experiences of a lifetime. Life was carefree and all about making friends and having fun; going to football games and parties and just being a student. I loved. As I walked through school to my locker, in between classes, I used to look at some of the young ladies on the cheerleader team and say, "Wow! They are so popular... they have it going on." I didn't realize then that everyone had his or her own masked issues.

After school, the real fun began. I grew up in an area of Chesapeake that was known as the "hood" or "projects." While I was poor and looked down on by many, I didn't even realize it. It was in the projects that I formed great friendships and experienced the joy of community. It was a carefree way of living.

My evening routine usually consisted of sitting on my porch watching the cars go by and waving at people. We lived on the main street, so people had to come pass our house, which led to exciting nights of observing their comings and goings. After awhile, I got to know everyone's car. Chesapeake proved to be a huge adjustment for us city slickers. In New Jersey, my siblings and I were used to being able to walk to the corner store to get candy, now the nearest store was 2-3 miles away!

Like many young children, I enjoyed watching the popular evening tv shows with my mother. Intrigued by the characters I saw on the screen, I'd consistently asked her, "How did those people get on tv? How did those people become rich? How can I become rich?" Her response to me was always the same reply, "We are not the privileged. Stuff just don't happen to us like that."

In bed at night, I would always ask God how he could give them that privilege and my family had to work so hard. As I sought to escape my reality, I began to immerse myself in reading books. Books took me to locations that I said I would never visit because we didn't have money and were not on the privilege list.

In school the next day, I decided that I was going to stop people from putting the label of "nerd" on me by getting involved in extra-curricular activities. At that time I was much taller than most of the young ladies in my ninth grade class. I remember walking down the hall and having the basketball coach walk up behind me. She asked, "Have you ever played basketball before?" I said, "No" and she said "Cool, you are now on the girls varsity basketball team." Shocked, I replied, "okay."

That afternoon, I was bursting with excitement and couldn't wait to get to the house and tell my parents. As I broke through the door, I hurriedly told my mother what the coach said and that I was now on the basketball team. She could hear the excitement in my voice. Surprisingly, my mother replied, "What do you know about basketball? You don't know how to play that. Don't get out there and embarrassed us." I was crushed. I wanted to hear my mother proclaim, "That's great baby, do your best!" Unfortunately, I did not receive the positive reinforcement that I desired.

My father was not consistent. All I knew was that my dad drank a lot. It was never explained to me that my father was an alcoholic and that was a disease. We had our good days; when he would joke and we would laugh and he would be the life of the party. Then, there were those days when he would get drunk and pick fights with my mom and the shouting matches would begin. It seemed like they went on for hours! When the shouting began, I would retreat to my books and reading or practicing and playing basketball. They were my refuge.

Having basketball practice was one of the highlights of my week. I loved this time because the coach would encourage me and recommend books for me to read. It really blew me away that this stranger was encouraging me and lifting me up in the way that I desired my family to. I didn't understand it, but it worked. The library became my sanctuary. I couldn't get enough of reading and was soaking it up like a sponge.

Friday night was game night. This was always a highlight for me. For four hours I was somebody, I was #15. As my skills increased, I began to start in some games. On this particular night, I had the privilege to start for the team. Running up and down the court, I played as hard as I could. Every now and then I'd hear someone call out my name and cheer me on. For me, this was heaven. After a quick foul, I found myself at the free throw line. Already slightly nervous, I heard my dad yell "Baby, you've got this!" Immediately, the nerves took over my center-stage body. As everyone looked at me, anticipating my shots, I was consumed by embarrassment. I started believing those words my mom said, "We are not the privileged." and "Stuff just don't happen to us like that."

Even though my dad had his issues, one thing I could count on was his support at my Friday games. He was there, cheering me on, drunk and all. After awhile, he become a normal fixture on the bleachers. That embarrassment became pride, as other kids would walk up to me and say, "Even though your dad is drunk, at least he is here supporting you... I don't know where my dad is."

We may not have had the latest clothes or gadgets, but we were wrapped in love, had food to eat and a warm house to call home. Those four years of high school started out slow, but with time, I slowly evolved into another person. I started my freshman year with low self- esteem and never thought I was good enough to be around certain people or do certain things. I remember admiring the girls with the long flowing hair and wishing that I was like them.

Once I found out that reading was empowering, I read every magazine that came to the house, from cover to cover, just to gain the knowledge. The more I read, the more I thirsted for more. The more I read, the more I realized that whatever I wanted in life, I had to go after it. I had to make a plan and go for it. I would soon find this to particularly be true, as I shifted locations again.

After graduating from high school and moving into adulthood, I made another relocation. The moment that changed my life occurred when I moved from Jacksonville, NC to Enfield, NC. After finding employment and getting my twin babies into pre-kindergarten, life got busy. Even though I began to settle into my newly found life, I knew there was more to life than my current situation, I just couldn't put my finger on it. I prayed one evening, "Lord it has to be more to life than working, picking kids up from school and heading home to do it all over again."

The following morning, as I was picking up the mail, there was a magazine and on the cover were four beautiful women talking about how their life changed when they became business owners. They talked about joining a home-based business that allows individuals to start their own travel company. I was impressed by the unlimited opportunity for growth. Unlike my job, there was no glass ceiling. This magazine was my introduction to the world of Network Marketing.

I started to seek out the women on the cover through email and social media. I had questions and I wanted someone to answer them. I also knew that I had a story to share and wanted to become an author, so I reached out to a young lady, on facebook, and asked a couple questions about self-publishing. She was a wealth of information. I have learned that whatever you want to do, you simply need to find someone who is doing it and has expertise and seek them out. Never be afraid to ask questions, in order to gain clarity and insight on something that you want to do.

With the phenomenal personal development trainings and opportunities, I have grown as a person in this industry. Through this vehicle, I have met people that are now everlasting friends. We have established diverse and unbreakable bonds. Just being able to talk with like-minded individuals who have dreams and goals and want more in life is priceless.

As I talked with women in my age group and I realized that we are mothers, wives, and wear so many other hats that we have forgotten about ourselves. Some of us believe that it's too late to achieve our dreams. Because of this, I decided to birth my business *Spark Your Passion,* where we uncover the gifts that you have buried within and begin to unwrap them and share them with the world. I also self-published a book, *Courage 2 Take The SHOT,* because the women that I talked to or encountered on facebook, were scared to go after their dreams. I wanted to let them know that if a 52-year-old woman can do it, so can you. You truly have to believe in yourself and unleash yourself from the bonds of negativity in your life. As long as you are still breathing there is life left in you to pursue whatever your heart desires.

There are many days that you will get tired, but if you have a big enough WHY in front of you, you will be motivated to persevere. You have to have your Mind, Body and Spirit intact to leave a Legacy.

What I Have Learned: Wisdom From A SHERO

- **Pray Daily, Exercise, Meditate and drink plenty of water!**

- **Take care of your vessel.** This is what I know from experience; if you don't take care of this vessel, that we call a body, then you are not going to be able to pursue anything because your body will let you know.

- **You must have the right mindset.** You have to get your mindset right in order to step into this world of entrepreneurship. Read up on what rich people do and how they became successful. If you like Oprah, read about her, if you like Steve Harvey read about him. I learned, much later in life, that reading and knowledge go hand in hand. Once you read something, no one can take that away from you. Millions of dollars are hidden in books, but we as a people will never get it if we don't read.

- **Learn the POWER of leaving a LEGACY!** Now legacy is a word that I just recently started to understand fully. Michael Jackson is a perfect example of legacy; his children's children will never have to work a day in their life., if they don't want to. You want to be able to leave a presence on this earth to signify that you were here. Yes, memories are great, but as you get older, your memories will fade. We have one chance, while here on earth, to do something that outlives us. Everything I do; from writing books and having businesses, is to leave a legacy for my last name. That is what's remembered. So understanding that what you are doing is meaningful and years from now people will be talking about what mom or grand mom did.

- **Spend time in spiritual renewal.** When it comes down to the spirit, I am a Christian and I have to spend time praying and listening. Whatever you do for your spirit requires time and dedication; that is where clarity is revealed and you receive answers to your questions and guidance to direct your path.

My favorite scripture is Ephesians 3:20: *Now to Him who is able to do exceedingly abundantly above all that we ask or think, according to the power that works in us!*

- **It is worth it!** It's time for us as a people to stop existing and start living. Never let your past mistakes or fears stop you from being all you can be. Often the struggle will be hard, but the reward will be well worth it!

Author Natasha Perry

Natasha embodies and demonstrates the profound principles of her wonderful parents- Willie and Barbara Perry. Their strong values played a fundamental role in her achievements, which include a Bachelor degree in Computer Science, Minor in Mathematics as well as a Graduate degree in Management Information Systems.

Natasha's altruism is evidenced in her community service, as she is an avid volunteer in her church and remains a strong advocate for helping women and children. She is smart, intelligent, strong, beautiful and more importantly she is kind to others and serves as an example for others to emulate and she REMAINS UNSTOPPABLE in her pursuits to make a positive change in our communities and a lasting legacy, demonstrating what can be achieved through perseverance, humility, wisdom and God's everlasting love.

Get to know Author Natasha Perry:

LinkedIn - https://www.linkedin.com/in/natasha-perry-88b26810

Traci Lynn Jewelry - www.tracilynnjewelry.net/natashaperry

Now We No Campaign- http://nowweno.net/#about

Nspire Network- http://nspirenetwork.com/empower

Natasha Perry

Unleashing A Marriage Unfulfilled

When I look back over my early life, it was pretty remarkable. I had a wonderful childhood with loving parents. I was their miracle child. I was born three months early and weighed only one and a half pounds at birth. I would like to tell you that I was just excited about entering this world, but the real story is that my mother was suffering from preeclampsia. That is why I was born early. The doctors didn't expect me to survive, but God had other plans! I had a purpose.

I attended college at Fayetteville State University and received a degree in Computer Science and then received a Master's degree from North Carolina A&T University in Management Information Systems. I had a good job and had purchased my first home at the age of 26. I considered myself doing well. Then life happened. Things were going fairly well until that day in May of

2010 when I stepped outside and saw my ex-boyfriend moving in four houses down from me. I lived in a townhouse at the time, so that was way too close for comfort. He and I had a nasty break up in 2009 and he would pop up at my house trying to get me back. I had to threaten him with a restraining order to deter him from continuing to bother me. For a while I didn't hear anything from him. So, seeing him moving in was a total shock. It also made me wish I had placed that restraining order on him. If I had, I wouldn't be seeing this right now.

About a month after my ex moved in, I had another new neighbor move in next door to me. I wasn't sure if I wanted to introduce myself because the guy looked mean. A few weeks later, I saw him on my way into the house and I did speak to him. I also ended up speaking to his mother. She sat on the porch for two hours talking to me. She was telling me that he was a great guy and that she thought we would get along. Supposedly, he loved God and was a family oriented man. I started to think that maybe my first impression of him was incorrect and I should give him a chance. Now in hindsight, I realize that she was just talking him up because she was trying to get him out of her house. I ran into him a few days later and we started talking. He seemed like a nice guy and what he said seemed to line up with what his mother had shared. Since I was still dealing with my ex-boyfriend living so close, I decided that it would be good to at least make a friend. Hopefully, he would be able to protect me if I needed it. I wasn't attracted to him, but he seemed nice.

After talking for a few weeks, we started to officially date. For the first few months everything was great. We spent a lot of time together and he treated me very well. He was always very polite and I was a priority for him. After about five months of dating, he proposed. At the time, I was very excited, yet shocked that it had happened so suddenly. I knew he said that he always wanted to be married, but I was quite the opposite. Being married wasn't a lifelong dream for me, but I thought he loved me and had the best intentions for me. I told my family about the engagement and they were happy, but also nervous. My mother asked me,

"How are you going to keep up your current lifestyle once you marry him?" She knew that he was a truck driver and he didn't make as much money as I did. My naïve answer to her was, "Well, I make enough money to pay everything now. So, why would my lifestyle change after I'm married? He should just be adding to it." I would later find out the answer to that question the hard way.

We were married in 2011. Instantly, things became different. Literally, the first day of being a wife was a horrible experience and I knew that I had made a terrible mistake. I spent my first night as a wife alone because he decided to go watch a boxing match at his cousin's house. I spent the entire night crying. He showed me from the beginning that I no longer mattered. He got his wife and that was all that he wanted. My wants and needs were no longer a priority. I guess he figured that he could do whatever he wanted because we were now married. He knew that I was a Christian with strong beliefs; so, he didn't think I would leave him. It all went downhill from there.

Three months after we got married I lost my job due to a company merger. The strange part was that I wasn't too sad about losing my job. I just knew that God had everything under control and that there was no reason to stress out. God always provides. I received a decent severance package and I was also eligible for unemployment. Since I was the main breadwinner, things were definitely tight financially for a while. After six months of unemployment, I received a job at a non-profit company. I was able to gain a lot of skills at this job, but it was $17,000 less than what I was making at my last job. Through it all, I kept praying that God would repair my marriage. It seemed like the more I prayed the worse it got. Being a truck driver, he was hardly ever home and even when he was at home, he was out all night like he was still single. He did whatever he wanted, but I was supposed to always remain at home. I felt like a slave in my own home. My only purpose was to satisfy him. Even the time that I spent with my family was a problem. I only saw my family about once a month and I would schedule those visits during the times that he was at work. I tried to always be home when he was at home. He became more and more jealous of my family. He would call me when I was with them and tell me that I needed to come home because he was on the way home. I would leave my family and make the two-hour drive back home. When I got back he would go out with his friends and leave me alone. It wasn't about him wanting to spend time with me it was about controlling with whom I spent my time. He would even get upset if I dressed up. He would say, "People are going to be looking at you wondering why you are with me?" Most men would be happy to see their wife taking good care of herself and looking attractive, because we are an extension of each other. I had an opportunity to be in a commercial for the computer school that I attended. He didn't want me to be in the commercial because too many guys would see me and would try to 'holla' at me. The insecurity ran deep with him.

We argued all the time. It had gotten so bad that I began drinking in order to tolerate being with him. I started going into a depression, and I didn't even realize it at the time. All I knew was that I was fatigued and losing weight. I started having a recurring dream about dying. My dream depicted us together in a car driving and crashing over a cliff. I started having the dream more and more frequently. I believe that was God telling me that I needed to leave. My prayers started changing from, "Please Lord, repair my marriage." to "Please Lord, show me what you want me to do." If leaving is the answer, then give me an exit strategy."

Another way that God nudged me in the right direction was through my cousin Kortney. One day she said to me, "I don't want to visit you in the hospital. You are always so stressed out and that isn't good for your health." She was growing more and more concerned about me. It didn't help that I had a party at my house one day that ended up with me crying for an hour because a friend asked me how I was doing. Yes, it was getting increasingly worse. Kortney was so afraid to leave me that day. The other person that helped me was my cousin, Desiree. She came to visit me one day and when she got back home she sent me a text asking me if I was okay. I laughed and asked her why she asked that question. Apparently, I still thought that I was hiding the pain I was carrying around. She told me that my house had a very sad and dark feeling. She said that I didn't seem like the same person and something just felt wrong. Prior to that day, I had never told anyone what was happening in my marriage. I was told during pre-marriage counseling that you should keep whatever is going on in your marriage between you and your spouse. I had a conversation with Desiree and Kortney. Both had the same response. They told me that they didn't condone divorce, but I needed to get out. Even though I had a thousand reasons to leave, I wanted to make sure I did everything I could to try to save the marriage. I tried marriage counseling. Two separate counselors said I was in an unhealthy marriage and needed a trial separation. I told myself that if I missed him at all during the separation or if he gave me a reason to stay, then I would stay.

I didn't miss him at all and he definitely didn't give me a reason to stay. Even serving him the divorce papers was an ordeal, but I finally got them signed. That was the best feeling; but it was bitter sweet. I didn't get married thinking I was going to get divorced. I respect marriage and would rather have had it work. There are times when you need to know when to walk away. I also want to mention that since my divorce I haven't had another death dream. That was truly a sign from God.

Even after the divorce, it wasn't an easy path to recovery and wholeness. I was mentally and emotionally broken. I was watching a show on TV and it said that the best way to help yourself was to help others. When you are helping others, your issues don't seem so big. I decided to give it a try. I joined the Ray of Hope Ministry at my church. It is a ministry that helps homeless people and others that are less fortunate. I donated boxes of food and half of the clothes in my closet to the ministry. It was a satisfying feeling. The more I worked with the ministry, the better I felt. It turns out it was a ray of hope for me! In the words of Mahatma Gandhi, "The best way to find yourself, is to lose yourself in serving others."

In 2015, a year after the divorce, I got an awesome job opportunity. I ended up getting the same salary that I had in 2012.

That was definitely a huge blessing. Since my ex and his mother lived next door to me, it was very uncomfortable. I began praying that they would move, but it was apparent that was not going to happen. Then I started praying that God would allow me to move. A former neighbor was a real estate agent. I decided to reach out to him. He was so excited to assist me. We put the house on the market in January of 2016 and it sold the next day! Look at God!!!! When I say God had a right now blessing for me, I almost couldn't believe it. The next part was finding a new home before my closing date. We looked at a few homes and then I found "The One". It was a beautiful home. I put an offer on it and it was accepted. Things were really headed in the right direction. I closed on my new home March 10, 2016. I believe in the biblical meaning of numbers. So, March is 3, which means Divine Completeness and 10 means Testimony. I thanked God for all the blessings that he has bestowed upon me. Now, I am in a place in my life where I can help others. I still work with different outreach organizations including my sorority, Alpha Kappa Alpha Sorority, Inc. and I assist my family and friends with whatever I can. I am also a part of a campaign called Now We No. It is a movement that spreads the awareness of issues that are caused by the feminine products currently on the market and offers a healthy alternative. We, as women, will no longer have to suffer in silence. I believe we are blessed in order to be a blessing to others. Always remember, "Don't be afraid to start over. It gives you a chance to build something even better."

What I Have Learned: Wisdom From A SHERO

- **Always put your trust in God and allow him to guide your way.**
- **Don't marry potential!** – Accept him 'as is' and don't think you can change him. You may be expecting more than he is capable of providing you.
- **Don't date from a place of brokenness.** – Broken people attract broken people. Learn to love yourself first.
- **The best healing comes from serving others.**

Author Kimberly Perry-Sanderlin

Kimberly Perry-Sanderlin was born and raised in Northeastern NC (Bertie County) and takes pride in her hometown upbringing. After graduating from The University of North Carolina-at Chapel Hill with dual degrees in Sociology and Elementary Education, she started her professional career in Greensboro, NC. At press, Kimberly is embarking on a new professional journey; excitedly starting her 11th year of education in the Raleigh- Durham area.

Over the past 5 years, Kimberly found her professional passions in the area of teacher mentorship, flipped/blended learning, and curriculum development. With the support of her retired educator parents, Kimberly became CEO/Co-Founder of SynergyEd Consulting Group. Her vision is to create and implement quality educator training worldwide through 21st century tools.

Kimberly is one who does not shy from pursuing all of her passions. She is a National Board Certified Teacher (2013), a NC Kenan Fellow (2013-14), and Fulbright-Hays Group Project Abroad to China participant (2015). In addition, Kimberly is a budding photographer; providing all photography for Sisters Lifting Sisters and the *Unleash Your Shero* project.

Kimberly's current projects include developing a daily vocabulary program (Rapid Root Challenge) and completing her memoir ("God's YESS Through My Mess"- Spring 2018 release). When Kimberly is not wearing her educator or photographer hats, she enjoys quality time with family (especially her 5 year old prince, Chauncey and niece, Camryn), cooking, dining, reading, and traveling.

Get to know Author Kimberly Perry-Sanderlin: SynergyEdConsulting.com

Kimberly Perry-Sanderlin

Unleashing My Power After Divorce

I'd rather have bad times with you, than good times with someone else

I'd rather be beside you in a storm, than safe and warm by myself

I'd rather have hard times together, than to have it easy apart

I'd rather have the one who holds my heart

~ Luther Vandross

The lyrics from this iconic song were the first thing that would play in my mind when my husband and I would have a scuffle. I didn't find it odd that it was lyrics before Bible verses. Even though most that know me will tell you that there's no greater love in my life than the love I have for God. I've always had an intense connection with music. At times, it was the music that would make things clearer... as if the lyrics were aligning with my faith... as if they were sent from God. If I were going through a tough situation, the next song on the radio would speak to my spirit, and send me to the Bible and on my knees to get confirmation from the Lord.

Since an early age, music became the love language that connected me to God. And that's what I thought initially when these Vandross lyrics began creeping into my daily subconscious. But the more those lyrics were on repeat in my head, I realized that just as lyrics can be prophetic and of God; they can also be used by the enemy. Each time that something would occur in my marriage that I questioned, I'd hear the lyrics replay clearly in my subconscious and I'd tell myself "this is just the devil trying to get in the way" or "maybe I'm overreacting." It was as if the enemy used something that I held dear- my musical life connection- to brainwash me into thinking everything was "okay" when it was far from that. By the time I realized what was happening, I was cleaning up blood stains from my carpet and on the brink of insanity. How did it all come to this?! How did childhood love (with the 8th and 12th grade prom pictures to prove it) go from being enraptured lovers to enraged enemies, in what seemed like overnight?

To even begin to understand, I must pause the climax and take you back almost 20 years. It was June 1998 when I met my future husband at 4-H camp. At the time, he was just one of the crew; the oldest of 3 brothers attending the camp together. Since his 4-H agent and mine were close, we ended up experiencing camp activities together. What's ironic was that I had a huge crush on another camper at the time, and my future husband helped me orchestrate encounters with this crush... never realizing that our friendship and chemistry were budding; even at a young age. We became pen pals and phone buddies after camp.

You'll have to wait for the memoir to fill in all the gaps... just know that our puppy love and common experiences further developed over the years. Add memories... from 12th grade prom night... to a tough break-up prior to college... to us both helping each other maneuver college relationships with others... we continued to be drawn to each other. Even though we were both from different sides of the railroad track; me from a supportive middle class family and him from forced independence and poverty- we were able to grow together. It was his independence and ability to "get things done" that continued to draw me closer to him... he was what I wasn't and what I needed. We'd have conversations all night about the sociological theory that we were both learning. We'd become each other's' best friend, lover, and supporter... what I thought made the "perfect" couple. We both graduated and had dreams and goals for building a life together. And why wouldn't it work?! We'd grown to know and respect each other... we were open and honest about our dreams and aspirations and how we could achieve them... our chemistry was AMAZING! We ignored any objections from either side of our family and professed our love and commitment to one another on August 23, 2008. Until the birth of our son, it was the happiest day of my life...

Fast forward back to the worst day of my life... my 11-month old son screaming "mommy!" incessantly... me crying uncontrollably and telling my child through a closed door that "everything was alright…" all while in a manic state; attempting to feverishly scrub out the blood from our white carpet. Everything was NOT "alright!" I was clearly on the cusp of a psychotic break… while my husband was driving himself to the emergency room.

It took me a few minutes more of scrubbing the floor to come back to reality. I momentarily couldn't process the need to stop scrubbing the floor to calm my screaming child. After calming our son and getting him to bed, I called my husband. I thanked God that he even answered and apologized and begged him to "forgive me." Within hours, he was home with 11 visible stitches where I had stabbed him in malice. But why?

Was it because I had just caught him brazenly talking to another woman in our home? Was it because I'd recently discovered that he'd been stealing money from my personal bank account for months; continually causing deeper financial debt, for which I was left solely responsible to rectify? Was it because our marriage was now devoid of affection and intimacy; withheld by him out of spite and withheld by me due to sheer exhaustion from mentally and financially supporting most of our household responsibilities? Was it because he continued to secretly abuse alcohol while refusing to get proper help? Was it because he let his frustrations out on me consistently through passive-aggressive, emotionally-abusive interactions?

It wasn't until I began my own divorce recovery that I began to get the answers to these questions. Now, on the other side of victory, I know that the roots of our dysfunctional marriage ran much deeper than my husband's singular contributions. By truly opening myself up to God to RESTORE in the midst of my brokenness, I was blessed with supernatural clarity. One of the first things that I realized was my own volatility due to years of emotional abuse and neglect. Because my own heart had become hardened as my marriage crumbled, those external to my marriage became casualties of war. My parents and elder sister bore the brunt of my wrath. Many times, I lashed out at them even though they were the main ones financially supplementing my household and giving unconditional love when it was definitely not deserved, because of my unkind behavior. I also realized that I had been an enabler in our marriage; from preparing his resumes, to paying all the bills and making all the repairs- I had unfairly lightened his load to the point that he became complacent. The biggest thing that I learned was if God is not first in both spouses' lives and the center of the marriage, it becomes an uphill battle. I also learned that one can't solve anyone else's issues; growth comes from honest, consistent introspection and WORK.

For me and my ex-husband, the explosive night in 2013 proved to be the nail-in-the-coffin of our marriage. In an attempt to restore our marriage, we both tried individual and couples counseling. Unfortunately, the physical and emotional scars that had been compounded, proved too deep to be repaired at this stage in our lives. However, for anyone in a similar situation of spousal abuse, know that there still is hope for your recovery and even your marriage.

What I Have Learned: Wisdom From A SHERO

- **Abuse is abuse**: Surprising to some, the most damning abuse to me in my marriage was the financial abuse. In retrospect, I realized that the years when my husband was stealing from my personal account were what caused me to begin to question my sanity. Each time that he acted as if he didn't know why our "bill money" was short made me second-guess my financial competency. Each time that a piece of jewelry went missing- that he later admitted to pawning- I would question myself. Perhaps I had not placed them where I knew they'd been placed. Each incident silently chipped away at my own sanity... Before I knew it, I was a shell of the confident, level-headed person that I had once been. On a daily basis, I dreaded going home. Work was something that I could control. I never knew if I would be coming home to Dr. Jekyll or Mr. Hyde. After the separation, I began to see myself clearly again in the mirror; literally and figuratively. Even though those closest to me would hint to it, I didn't notice that I'd lost 15 pounds. When I was once again able to financially afford my professional stylist, she discovered 2 sizeable bald spots hidden in my natural coif. This is when I finally realized that stress and emotional abuse is REAL!

- **There is no gender cap on abuse**: I'm pretty sure some readers initially assumed that I was cleaning up my own blood in the climactic scene. That is because in our society there are many myths about abuse. Whether it's the myth that men don't get abused, or that the only abuse is when someone physically harms another, these myths cause people to second guess-abuse... ultimately resulting, many times, in life-threatening or fatal situations.

- **Seek counseling**: My husband and I separated on December 28, 2015 and I was in counseling on January 7, 2016. Having counseling early on made all the difference in my recovery. For me, it was important that I have both spiritual and pragmatic counseling. So I simultaneously committed to Divorce Care sessions and private counseling. Divorce Care taught me not to be ashamed of my need for divorce; even reminding me of God's need to divorce the church (Jeremiah 3:8). Understanding God's continuous love beyond my own transgressions proved key to my spiritual recovery. Private counseling allowed me time to dissect my explosive anger, and to truly pinpoint how it affected my marriage and other relationships.

It is also important to seek counseling for any children involved. I recommend both the Divorce Care Program (13-weeks) and Divorce Recovery Program (10-weeks). There is also a Divorce Care 4 Kids (DC4K) program.

If you feel that you are capable of self-counsel (rare!), begin your process by pinpointing your role in the dysfunction of your marriage. It takes two to tango in all aspects of a relationship...

- **Get out**: If counseling and spiritual advisement do not help remedy the issues, don't fear separation. Sometimes being apart will be motivation for both parties to heal and possibly reconcile. However, NEVER feel guilty about the need for separation; sometimes it is the safest choice.

- **Forgive yourself and ask for forgiveness**: Once I was past my own anger, I genuinely asked my ex for forgiveness. This wasn't for him; but for me. Until you repent to God (#1) and ask for forgiveness for your role in the demise of your marriage, you will not be free to move on and grow from the experience.

- **Avoid "band-aids"**: The biggest error that you can make during your recovery is entertaining another love interest. I call these rebound situations "band-aids" because you're only temporarily finding comfort. Until you fully address the issues at hand (dysfunction), it will become a cyclical part of your life. A great book to help you on this journey is *The Wait* by DeVon Franklin and Meghan Goode.

- **Develop yourself**: Use this time to RECOVER and REBUILD yourself. Find out what you truly enjoy. Now is the time to develop a solid 1/3/5-year plan and start executing! Especially if children are involved, you need to think about ways that you can diversify your income while maximizing your time. You also want to spend your time thinking about the qualities that you need and want in a future mate. I recommend reading *5 Love Languages* by Gary Chapman.

- **Put your faith in God**: My biggest fear in stepping out of my marriage was the potential financial impact. But because I remained faithful in developing my personal skills and expertise, within a year, I was in a better financial state than I'd ever been during my marriage. This situation has taught me to PRAY and K.I.M. (Keep it Moving) because God's got it!

You Have The
Power To
Unleash Your SHERO

Author Tyeasia Kiah

Tyeasia Kiah is a native of Tarboro NC. Tyeasia is a mother of a beautiful daughter Kali'yah Dorsey. Tyeasia is the proud author of two literary works; *The Battle Is Not Yours* and *Say It Loud*.

Tyeasia is a motivational speaker, empowering women fighting mental illness, and owns two businesses; Fierce Creations, a beaded jewelry designs company and Fierlous Girls Inc. a mentoring program for young girls. A strong community leader, Tyeasia strives to motivate and empower women and young girls to understand that their pasts do not weaken their futures; rather allows them to grow and become stronger!

Get to know Author Tyeasia Kiah:

www.fierlousgirlsbyty.com

http://tyeasiak.wixsite.com/fierlousgirlsinc

Tyeasia Kiah

Unleashing Mental Illness

Ever felt like you were looking at your life through another pair of lens? I was lost, not knowing if I was coming or going. I was going from happy and smiling to a rush of sadness and a shutdown of feelings. In 2012, I was diagnosed with Major Depressive Disorder and PTSD. However, my problems came long before the diagnosis.

I had a loving family which provided me with my necessities and when possible, much more. While I didn't go without, I was raised in a home where "I love you" was not passed around as it should have been. These words were not used and affection was not shown unless someone died in the family. Even then, the affection was short lived; it faded away as the pain of the death subsided. "I love you" is what I needed from my family. Not having it caused me to seek attention and compliments such as " you are beautiful", from men and friends.

As adults, we forget that love and affection starts at home first. "Thank you," and appreciations start at home. If lacking affection, a child goes into the world seeking it from all the wrong people and places. They find themselves empty on the inside. I did not like myself; my skin color, my skin texture, my weight, my lack of proper hygiene, or my voice.

Being bullied decreased my self-esteem and self-confidence tenfold. It never let up. I was ridiculed every day, about something! If it wasn't girls trying to fight me for not standing up for myself or being too quiet, it was guys talking about my voice and the fact that I had really bad acne. Let me not forget, not understanding that my thick-coiled hair could cause odor, I was ridiculed for that. Although I had friends in high school, nothing compared to the torture and torment I experienced each day on the school bus ride and on the school campus.

My first suicide attempt was in the 10th grade. I was talked about so badly! I was constantly under attack! There came a time when I felt that I could no longer deal with the humiliation. I just wanted a permanent peace. However, God had other plans for me; plans that at my young age I could not see or comprehend.

Although God had other plans for me, I still had to go through other trials and tests to see if I was strong enough to stand the fight. When I went to college I had very few friends because I felt like everyone was against, or talking about me. I was extremely paranoid and dealing with low self-esteem and lack of confidence. When I did make friends, my communication skills were horrible; meaning I could not express my concerns in an appropriate way to my friends. Frustrated, I would isolate myself for days or weeks. You see, Major Depressive Disorder will have you feeling fine one minute and sad and lonely the very next. Those of us who suffer from this disorder, do not realize that we are causing our own loneliness by shutting people out of our lives. Major Depressive Disorder takes over your life to the point that normal activities are adversely affected, such as hanging with family or friends, or performing well in your occupation.

During my first year of college I almost failed because I hardly attended class. Not understanding the coursework, and isolating myself to the point that I could not reach out for help, caused my GPA to plummet to a 0.8 GPA. I was put on academic probation. I was heartbroken and did not know which way to turn. I did not know what my purpose was in life, but with God's help, today I am learning day by day. I lost friends, during my college years; lost myself, but pulled myself together and finished school; graduating with my bachelor's degree.

After college, my destructive patterns continued to follow me. I was trying to find love and peace in all the wrong places. I was dating and sleeping with almost every man I talked to; not knowing I was transferring the negative, nasty spirits they had been carrying onto myself. I had no sense of self. I was looking for acceptance and happiness in men and friends when I needed to look within myself and ask God for guidance.

When I felt like my whole world had come to an end, I finally decided to make a change. I was engaged and the wedding was called off just two weeks before our wedding date because I could not come to peace with loving myself and being content with one man. I fell into an even deeper depression when this relationship ended. I knew that I wanted to change. I desperately wanted to get help; I just didn't know how to get help or why it was so important at that point. As I said before, I lost friends because of my depression. I would turn my nose up at others and avoid talking to them for days. Eventually, many of my friends, tired of my unexplainable behavior and released me from their lives. While this caused another dark tunnel for me, I knew it was me who couldn't get it right.

There I was, without a man, having few friends, and losing my mind! So, what was left to do? I tried committing suicide again. I cut my family off and just went into a deeper, darker hole. I was lost. I stopped going to church because I just couldn't understand why it was me who was going through so much, or why I was still here. At the time, I felt like church folks were hypocrites and gossipers; they were not really God's children or helping those in need. I went to a traditional church where all they talked about was backsliders, whores, gossipers, and liars. Instead of helping individuals who were in those categories, they were just talked about and treated as outsiders. I did not have to be a Christian to know that God was not pleased with the church work that was being done. So, you see, when you do not even feel safe or comfortable in church, what do you do? Well, I went back to what was normal for me, sleeping with this one and that one, isolating myself, going to work to keep the lights on and taking care of my child. I never neglected my responsibilities. However, my destructive behavior caused me to neglect myself and my family.

I know you are probably wondering; about the PTSD. I still haven't mentioned how or when I faced my traumatic ordeal. Well, here it is. My PTSD stems from two things; the first was a rape when I was just 12 years old by guys I thought were cool and were my friends. At the time, I did not understand rape. I thought if a girl said no, it just meant she was being hard to get, or so that was what I was told by guys. Being inappropriately touched by not one guy, but two, was not the way I wanted my first time to be. Shouting, "NO" repeatedly, was not how I expected it to be.

At the time, I did not think anyone would believe me. Firstly, because I was hanging with the fast girls I thought people assumed I had already had sex. Secondly, we were always hanging with guys, so why would anyone believe that I was a virgin and wanted to be different? I held my rape inside for over 11 years, until I was 23 years old. Sadly, I encountered these guys multiple times growing up, as they were my brother's friends. No one knew my secret. I never said a word. Whenever they came around, I would just leave or walk away.

Finally, the time came when I couldn't keep the rape a secret anymore. I was tired of walking around feeling like a whore, feeling unwanted, and being talked about to others when what was told was not true. Most importantly, I was tired of being trapped in my own mind; not being able to be honest about things, not feeling important or of value. My life was going in a negative direction because I felt as if the only way I would find love was through sex or what I could do for a man. I didn't know what love was. If I had truly understood love, maybe the rape would never have happened, or I wouldn't have been in that situation for it to occur.

My second traumatic experience happened when I was 16 and was in a serious car accident. I had just gotten my permit a few months prior and I was excited! I could go on the road on my own! On the night of the accident I was out, being fast, with my boyfriend. It was late and I missed my 9:00pm curfew. There I was, rushing to get my best friend and I home. I was going over the speed limit, and then it started raining. I hit a curve and the truck went spinning around in the road and landed in a ditch. I was in panic mode; I could not understand what had happened, and I was afraid to call my parents. Of course, when my mom arrived on the scene, she was very emotional and hugging me; checking to see if I was okay. However, my typical dad was very upset and said nothing to me for days. This made my emotions worse. Ever since then, I have been terrified to drive in the rain. I would literally pull over and wait for it to calm down or go as slowly as possible to get to my destination.

These traumatic experiences brought on my anxiety. I used to be afraid of everything; large crowds, speaking in large spaces, and accidents.

Thank God, I decided that my problems were greater than what I could handle on my own and my daughter deserved all of me, not just a part of me. I decided to seek counseling to be able to fully explore my problems and emotions and find ways of coping with them in a positive way. Yes, there are negative ways of dealing with past hurt and trauma such as sex, drugs, and alcohol. I did it all and I am not proud. I am just grateful that God has brought me through.

I started going back to church, reading, and praying and talking to God for myself. I realized that I needed to build a relationship with God for myself and not through my pastor or members of the church. That is when my life changed. God is still working on me. I am a work in progress; but I am doing it through Him. He is my light when I want to close all the blinds and lay in bed. He is my confidence when I hear the negative words of the bullies of the past. He is my salvation when I feel in bondage again. God is the one that can give me the love, attention, and guidance that I need, and the one that will never fail me... God. When I need to, I still seek counseling to stay strong, and I continue to pray and go to church.

I am now an author of two books; *The Battle Is Not Yours; A Fight To A Better Life*, and *Say It Loud, The Truth Hurts But It's A Soul Saver*. I am also a motivational speaker and business owner. My business, Fierce Creations has allowed me to birth my own t-shirt line and my nonprofit, Fierlous Girls Inc, allows me to provide much-needed mentoring to the community. I may not be where I want to be in my life, but I know that He has not given me the visions to fail!

What I Have Learned: Wisdom From A SHERO

- Know that God is with you and will guide you- In Psalms 37:4 it states that: *he will give you the desires of your heart* and Psalms 37:28 states *he will not forsaken his faithful children.* I believe in the word, and stand by it with my mustard seed of faith.

- Know that God will provide- Even when it seems dark and hopeless and you've tried everything, never lose faith. No matter what dark and ugly thing that you have been through; rape, abuse, self-hate, God can heal, restore, and make you whole again.

- NEVER GIVE UP!

Author Jasmine Cordell-Armstrong

Jasmine Cordell-Armstrong is a nationally certified, and licensed Recreation Therapist who graduated from East Carolina University in Greenville, North Carolina. She obtained a Bachelors of Science in Recreation Therapy. Later she would join the Breakpoint Coaching Collective, under the mentorship of Dr. Patrice Carter, to become a Certified Christian Life Coach. Upon completion of the Collective, she pursued her dream to launch "Heart of the Matter Coaching".

The vision of Heart of the Matter is to encourage, motivate, inspire, and equip women ages 13 and up to embrace their authenticity to become comfortable and confident in their skin; to propel them into their destiny, while resisting external pressures.

Heart of the Matter was birthed through her experiences, and interactions with other women. It was in those moments that she realized that everything she faced would bring meaning to life, and cause her to recognize the areas in her life that needed healing and restoration.

Get to know Author Jasmine Armstrong:

Website: https://www.heartofthemattercoaching.com
Email: heartrenovator@gmail.com
Facebook: @heartofthemattercoaching
Instagram: CoachJasmineAriel

Jasmine Cordell-Armstrong

Unleashing The Darkness of Grief

Lying at the feet, of my then Pastor in the midst of a prayer meeting; surrounded by familiar voices and people, I looked up from a place of desperation, brokenness, and surrender. All I could hear in my spirit was "for Your glory, I will do anything…" To no avail, repeatedly those words resonated in my spirit, so much that they sprung up out of the depths of my being to my lips. I began to sing aloud, "for Your glory, I will do anything".

Though this place was familiar territory to me, it was by far the deepest and darkest I had ever viewed it. I had a front row seat, better yet I was in the VIP section of depression, and I was uncertain if I would get out alive. Yet I thought, "how did I get here so fast, so hard and in so deep?"

This particular Saturday morning was not different from any other; however, on September 22, 2012 (one week to the day after turning 30 years of age) things changed. I was preparing to leave for class. I grabbed a few items, and headed out the door. No sooner than I arrived at class, my phone rang. The caller was my daddy's nurse asking me to come home. Immediately I thought to myself, "this man is being stubborn about something and I am the only one that can reason with him". This was frustrating because I had just arrived at class, for a final exam, and now I had to head home to "reason" with my daddy.

The entire drive I rehearsed in my head what I would say to my daddy, his reactions to my words, and my own reactions to his responses. I thought that once we finished with "business" I would make things more light-hearted by expressing to him that he had caused me to miss my final exam but thank you because it gave me extra time to study. Unfortunately, the conversation would not go in that direction at all. The speech that I spent 45 minutes preparing would not go as rehearsed. They were words that would not go past the gates of my mind and would never be had. Nothing could prepare me for the scene, harsh reality, and dialogue that I was about to venture into.

Feeling like I was in an episode straight out of a tv show, my mother, her friend, and I took the elevator up to my daddy's floor. I was making small talk but no one was truly responding to me. The doors opened, I stepped off the elevator, and everything fell quiet. Even though so much was going on around me, alarm bells, phones ringing and people talking; everything became hushed as if I was in a bubble looking out.

My heart began to race, I felt immediate panic, my hands became sweaty, my head swarmed, and I began to walk quickly to my father's hospital room. By this time a nurse caught up with me, had her hands around my shoulders, and was speaking to me eye-to-eye, face-to-face. I was unable to hear her. All I could hear was my own heartbeat, breaths, and thoughts saying, "I just need to get to him".

Woosh!!! "Honey did you hear me?"

"Honey, we did all we could, we worked on him for 45 minutes. I am so sorry but your father is gone. I am so sorry, he was such a nice man".

Immediately, my equilibrium was off; gravity was taken from under me. Again, people were talking but I could hear nothing. Faces became distorted, my body was hot, and the flood of tears did nothing to cool me down. In the blink of an eye, my world was turned upside down.

"What do you mean my daddy is gone? No! No! No! He just told me last night he loves me and he is proud of me". Little did I know those were the last words I would ever hear my daddy speak to me.

Finally stepping into the room, there he laid as if only asleep. And immediately I was the matriarch. No more time to cry, no time to think. Remain clear minded and help to make sound decisions. Bottle your tears and put a dam up for your emotions. Game face on.

The passing of my daddy would become the catalyst for a whirlwind of events to come as a result of the state of depression in which I would find myself.

The passing of my daddy led to my little family and I moving back home, with my then husband's parents, from the current city where we resided. This enabled me to assist my mother with getting on track, taking care of business affairs, healing, and learning how to maneuver a life without her life partner of 30 plus years.

Even though I was physically present my mind was now at a standstill. My mind was totally checked out. The morning I heard the words about my daddy passing, my life just halted. I became stuck in that very moment of time as if I was living in a loop. My heart was aching and I didn't know what to do with the pain and where to take it. So instead, I just held onto it.

Merely a shell of myself, I began to live less and less and only "existed" in this thing called life. I became emotionless and numb. From time to time, when the pain became too heavy, I would turn to my husband to share some of my hurt with him; though never enough to feel true release.

Aftermath

December 2012, my daddy had been passed for three months. With a shaky marriage that unraveled even the more, I had experienced a miscarriage right before Christmas (after an attempt for an abortion). I wasn't working, money was tight, and I was closing into myself even the more. My days and nights were meshing together and everything was dim and dark for me.

I stopped attending church and withdrew from spending time with family and friends. Since I had no true hobbies or outlets, everyday became a little harder to live. I began to drink more, and daily lived on bare minimum. I was now on auto-pilot.

By January of 2013, I had gotten my mother to where she needed to be to handle things on her own and I had stopped going over to see her every day, but was still available. I encouraged her to live a happy, free life; to travel and make new friends. In my mind I wanted her to do this so she would lose interest in having me around so much.

I began to feel my mind slip away and I was content with giving it over to the darkness that had now began to consume my very existence. I had already begun to plan my exit strategy. Depression became my safe place and best friend. Daily, it would sing me a melody to stay in the bed and at night it would scream at me to stay awake; to just hang out. No longer knowing up from down, I was in a downward spiral and a crash landing was inevitable.

The crash began and all controls began to go haywire leading up to my daddy's birthday (January 5th). By no means did I have any true buffers in place or plans of action to assist me with getting through this time. All I knew was that I had a bottle of vodka and needed a hand full of pills to marry with it. At this point, sleeping was to a minimum, thoughts and voices crashed around in my head nightly, and the noise needed to be turned OFF not down.

Sitting on the edge of the bed, I sent out a stream of "good-bye" and " I love you" text messages. A few calls came in, I ignored them and proceeded to find something to take, depression was choking me and now depression's cousin suicide was visiting with me. As I scavenged around the house looking for pills angel #1 was in route. Right as I reached the cabinet that normally housed medication, my brother walked in. My text and lack of response to his call prompted him to come to me. All I can remember is that my bottle of tears broke into a million pieces and I just wept and he held me. On that night he spoke life into me as well as saved my life.

I still was not in the clear because I still did not address and deal with everything in that moment. The same night, my then husband and I had an altercation (after my brother left), that led to my plane now crashing. May Day, May Day, all systems down! I grabbed my bottle of vodka and walked out the door into the darkness. I had blanked completely out. Angel #2 was dispatched and was led directly to me. Picking me up off of the side of the road my best friend prayed and sang to me. Then she took me and laid me on the altar.

In that moment, my dam had broken; the levy had been compromised and all I could do was look up out of the darkness and say, "No more, but for your glory I will do anything".

Between the death of my father, the death of my marriage, and the death of an unborn child, I was experiencing more than most. As a result, I was working to tackle untreated postpartum depression and major depression.

The night that I laid on the altar crying out, I knew that a change had to come and that I had to take back my mind. I then began to stand on the scripture Jeremiah 29:11 "For I know the plans I have for you," declares the Lord, "plans to prosper you and not to harm you, plans to give you hope and a future" (NIV). I began to seek help for myself, and day by day accept the circumstances around me.

Clearing Debris

In order to overcome and win each and every time my mind battled with depression, I fortified three important dimensions: *spirit, mind, and body*. I first began to strengthen my spiritual life and reorient it so that my mind and body could better heal. For me, a strong spirit is key. So I began to go back to church consistently, I was involved and serving. My greatest spiritual therapy is dance so I went back to ministering through dance at my church. I immersed myself in reading the Word as well as books that would bring edification to my spirit as well as my mind and give me tools to utilize as part of my daily practice.

Secondly, I cultivated my mind by participating in talk therapy with a counselor to work through the grief, to process very real and raw emotions. I joined a support group for separation and divorce. To help my mind, I also prayed and utilized biofeedback, relaxation, journaling, and mindfulness.

Upon stabilizing the first steps, I then worked on my body through diet and exercise. I started walking and then utilizing the *Couch to 5K* Program. I began to learn about foods that are high in alkaline and how they are beneficial. I researched and learned about what foods could trigger and/or influence your symptoms of depression. Lastly, I re-strengthened my community. I made my family and friends more aware of my condition, educated them, and began to temper the links that began to weaken during my state of reclusivity.

This process is like a equilateral triangle and if any side is lacking then the triangle loses its form, collapsing. In turn, leading me to begin to deteriorate mentally, emotionally, physically, and spiritually. Daily I have to work at keeping each process secure.

Since the passing of my daddy, and coming out of this particular place of darkness in my life; I still have had to confront depression and suicidal thoughts. Many people ask me how have you dealt with the passing of your daddy? How have you dealt with going through a divorce? How do you deal with depression?

I am honest and transparent in saying that I am just now, this year, fully coming out of the pain of my daddy passing away. I have reached this point through counseling and acceptance. As far as the divorce and depression goes, it's a day-by-day, moment-by-moment process practicing the tools aforementioned, but no matter what happens, I will keep pressing FORWARD!

What I Have Learned: Wisdom From A SHERO

- **Depression is not a death sentence** – It is nothing to be ashamed of nor should it be stigmatized. I live a full and joyous life now without medication (under the direction of my doctor), managed through talk therapy, the fortifying of my spirit, mind, and body and doing the things I love to do and you absolutely can too.

- **Strive each day to live intentionally and on purpose.**

- **Focus on strengthening your spirit, mind and body.**

Dedicated to: My daddy Johnnie Cordell Jr., remaining proud of me until the end. My mommy, Brenda Cordell, thank you for not letting anything stop you from loving me. Lovey, Allegro and Jaimica for being my angels. Ariana for being my biggest fan, loudest cheerleader, and motivation, and Colby for being my "Echo". To all those that feel they are alone, you aren't, and you can live STIGMA FREE

For resources, help, and information concerning mental health go to: https://www.nami.org/

You Have The Power To Unleash Your SHERO

Author Tilda Whitaker

Tilda Whitaker has over 25 years of nonprofit experience; 19 years as founder and director of a 501c3 nonprofit. Tilda has been trained as a Certified Christian Mentor and a Professional Credential Life Coach (PCC). Tilda is also a member of the International Coach Federation (ICF). She brings her own professional experience to bear; utilizing her ability to draw on her unique approach to using purpose as a catalyst for success to create unstoppable leaders who create legendary organizations.

Tilda is the CEO of P4 Coaching Institute where certified Christian mentoring and certified life coach trainings are provided. Tilda truly is a "Coach for the Coaches". She authored her first book *The Essence of God's Joy* in 2014 and co authored *Soul Source* in 2017. She is a Huffington Post spotlighted and bestselling author.

As Pastor of SOUL Winners International Ministries, Tilda carries an evangelistic emphasis and mantle. Her desire is to bring the body to truths and revelations that unlock fears of witnessing for the lost, instill zeal and energy in the hearts of believers and train leaders in the marketplace to accomplish at a higher level and ability.

Get to know Author Tilda Whitaker: p4coaching@gmail.com or www.p4cinstitute.com

Tilda Whitaker

Unleashing Your Purpose

My life today, as a purpose driven, self assured, faith walker is so different from being a shy, timid, underweight little girl who took a zero for not getting out of my seat in the 5th grade and giving an oral presentation from a paper I had written. I was petrified to speak. For a long time I didn't believe I had a voice.

I experienced a wealth of cultural diversity as a military brat; all needs met by protective, devoted parents who sheltered my siblings and me from the world. I was the only girl in the family so I was labeled spoiled. I had more than enough toys, and my mother, the homemaker made new, handmade outfits for me every week. I always described it as a good childhood. I was raised in the church, I attended Sunday School, served as an usher during my teen years and later worked full time as a church administrator for 12 years. I grew up in a denomination that taught that women served but were not heard. Women were not allowed to minister the gospel. These types of old-school church traditions contributed to keeping my voice subdued. Looking back at my life, I now realize that these were the things that tripped me up and tried to destroy my spirit.

There were many negative forces that came to hold me back and silence my greatness. The first was fear of failure. When I failed, it was particularly difficult for me to overcome and rebound. A second negative force was that I was so naive when I left home. While I had minimal life skills for survival, I was ill prepared to deal with the trickery of the wicked. I didn't know how to forge trusted relationships, outside of my family unit or even how to manage my personal finances. As a result, it was inevitable that I would stumble and fail, as I learned these life-lessons.

Many find themselves down in life when they face one trial. It might be that their marriage fails, or their home goes into foreclosure, or they lose their job, or they're parenting a small child all by themselves. There was one year that is deeply imprinted in my mind, as I wasn't struggling with just one of these life trials; I was overwhelmed by a long list of them. During this year, my dad had a heart attack, my grandfather died, I divorced, faced foreclosure, lost my transportation, lost my employment and tolerated bad relationships with men. I wasn't just "down"; I was deeply depressed, hopeless, humiliated, and in complete despair! The negative voice in my head was telling me that I wasn't going to make it out of this. I was fully convinced that this situation was entirely my fault. My low self-esteem and fear of speaking up for myself led me to repeatedly make bad decisions.

My devastating circumstances robbed me of my confidence. I no longer knew who I was or whose I was. I knew my parents loved me unconditionally and had taught me to live by faith, however, I feared that they did not really know me. They didn't see the Tilda that was failing in so many areas. Perhaps, their love was for the woman that God had purposed me to be.

During this time of my life, I didn't have a personal relationship with God, nor did I realize that I was fearfully and wonderfully made by Him. In sheer desperation, I isolated myself during this very dark time. For four months, I holed up at home, removing myself from the outside world, immersing myself in devotions, scriptures, Bible studies, and meditations. I arose in the morning with prayer; I wrote in my journal and had prayer in the noonday, and I prayed at night. I was intent on figuring out my purpose in life. Throughout my isolation process, I was fighting back against the self-doubts, the shame, guilt and the ever-encroaching darkness that threatened my progress. I knew God loved me, but was I worthy? I had lost so much and failed so spectacularly. Sometimes, when you need God the most, you also doubt Him the most.

One November night, the darkness in my head and heart tempted me with its promise of comfort, quiet, and an end to the guilt and shame. Letting the darkness completely swallow me seemed like the most peaceful option. I was weary of swimming upstream and I just wanted to stop flailing in water too deep for me. I wasn't cut out for this river and struggled with thoughts of gently floating to the bottom?

As I sat in the dark, my mind made up, I tried to decide? How did I want to go?

And we know that in all things God works for the good of those who love him, who have been called according to his purpose. — Romans 8:28

That night, on my knees, my answer came. He was near and He spoke to me. It was a clear voice. I heard it perfectly. Would someone else in the room have heard it? I think so; it was so clear and succinct. "You can't drown here," He said. "Swim." God told me to swim. And so I started swimming; toward life, toward the top, toward Him, processing my purpose. As I was swimming out of the darkness, it occurred to me that, as much as I had followed God and Jesus and loved His Word, all these years in the past, this time was different. As I shared with you earlier, I was one of generations of churchgoers and leaders, but that night was the beginning of the best and most beautiful thing in my life: – My PERSONAL RELATIONSHIP with God was sealed. Before this, I'd always believed in God, but I'd never had a real personal relationship with Him. I loved the church I grew up in and will always be thankful for the foundation and love I received there, but really walking with God was opening up a new kind of love for Him; a new kind of faith. It was beautiful and scary and real and magnificent. He and I were friends; I was his beloved. He didn't care about my past mistakes, my bad choices, or my revealed weakness during the previous weeks. He loved me. He was going to take care of me unconditionally!

That was the night I started processing my purpose. It became clear to me that I did have a voice, a mission and a message for other women suffering in the dark like I had. The chains of my self-doubt, my shame, and my guilt sloughed off as I floated to the top of the water. I grew stronger, the more I felt Him with me. I cut through the dark water and emerged at the surface. My mind was cleared. I didn't just hear Him, I felt Him. He embraced me and I embraced Him. Straight from His word, I was reminded of my spiritual journey.

My actual devotional read of that night was Ezekiel 47:2~

Man brought me back to the entrance to the temple, and I saw water coming from under the threshold of the temple toward the east (for the temple faced east). The water was coming down from under the south side of the temple, south of the altar. 2 He then brought me out through the north gate and led me around the outside to the outer gate facing east, and the water was trickling from the south side.

As the man went eastward with a measuring line in his hand, he measured off a thousand cubits[a] and then led me through water that was ankle-deep. 4 He measured off another thousand cubits and led me through water that was knee-deep. 4He measured off another thousand and led me through water that was up to the waist. 5 He measured off another thousand, but now it was a river that I could not cross, because the water had risen and was deep enough to swim in—a river that no one could cross. 6 He asked me, "Son of man, do you see this?"

Then he led me back to the bank of the river. 7 When I arrived there, I saw a great number of trees on each side of the river. He said to me, "This water flows toward the eastern region and goes down into the Arabah, where it enters the Dead Sea. When it empties into the sea, the salty water there becomes fresh. ʾSwarms of living creatures will live wherever the river flows. There will be large numbers of fish, because this water flows there and makes the salt water fresh; so where the river flows everything will live.

My suffering in the dark had not gone unnoticed by God; He had been there all along. As I was swimming to the top, out of the dark depths, I knew my purpose had something to do with helping other women swim out of the bottom of the dark waters.

In processing my purpose I eventually unleashed my SHERO, I learned life lessons. It became clear that failure is often a necessary part of success. I believe that behind every success story are embarrassing efforts, stumbling, setbacks and drastic changes of direction. I see now, that failure has been essential to processing my purpose.

As my relationship with God got personal, my internal SHERO strengthened. I stopped thinking I was insignificant. I realized that God truly has a plan for everyone; and indeed, He had a plan and purpose for me.

Through my own testimony, in 1998 I started a nonprofit with the mission to support single women through one-on-one mentoring and providing access to housing, employment and spiritual support. Over the years, thousands of single women have participated in formal funded services. Hundreds more have been referred to community service agencies. Services provided have been One-on-One Mentoring, WAVE Program (Women's Alternatives to Violent Expressions-the first state certified female abuser treatment program in Rocky Mount, NC. This program still thrives today), TOP Program- Licensed job training program, Life-Coping Skills Classes, SWIM's Healing Place-a state licensed transitional house for female ex-offenders, STOP-Stop the Offending Program-weekly on -site prison meetings , Information & Referral Center, resources-(food, transportation, school scholarships, clothing and child care assistance), weekly bible study, certified mentor training for over 500 women.(mentors have provided over 100,000+ volunteer service hours).

After generations of male ministers in our family, I broke belief systems, traditions and glass ceilings and became the first licensed, ordained female minister in our family. I found my voice!

What I Have Learned: Wisdom From A SHERO

Through my journey to process and understand my purpose, I asked God, in prayer, the following questions. Knowing, processing and walking in your purpose here on earth to unleash the SHERO within you. Ask yourself:

- **Who am I?-** Reflect on who you were as a youth. Consider your personal vision and what you wanted to be when you grew up.
- **What is your personal vision?-** What did you want to do when you grew up? What do you personally love? Know what career will fulfill you. What makes you feel alive?
- **Where are you from?-** What is your belief system? Ancestry? Understand your past experiences and learn to find the blessings in every test, trial and obstacle that you have overcome.
- **Why are you here?-** Know what you came here to do. You were gifted with unique gifts to contribute to the world. It's time to dig deep and pull them out.
- **Where are you going?-** What are your short and long term goals? What do you stand for?

I pray that you have started processing or will use these words to begin the process of **Unleashing your Purpose** and **Unleashing your SHERO.**

Let's pray together…

Lord, I surrender my life and everything I have to you. I want to do something, to lift, love and encourage others, not in my own strength, but by your strength. I know without you I can do nothing. I know my life is not my own, it is yours to work through me. Lord, I am grateful for this life you've given me. You've blessed me with different gifts and talents to unleash my SHERO. Help me understand how to cultivate those things to bring glory to your great name.

Amen

Author Helen Lawrence

Lady Helen is a native Floridian, a loving wife to a Retired Marine, a mother of three adult children and has five grandchildren. She is a Certified Life and Relationship Coach, Mentor, and Co-owner of Evolutional Coaching Services (ECS). She is a Meditation Practitioner, Visionary and Founder of the Woman II Woman Resource Outreach. She is also an Inspirational Speaker and Kingdom Facilitator. She is an Entrepreneur, a Multi-Media/Radio Personality and co-owner of Mocha LiVe Inspirational Media. Lady Helen aka "Lady Mocha;" hosts two internet radio shows with her husband; "Command the Morning" and Kingsmenship Strategies."

Lady Helen is a Minister, Author and Creative Magazine Columnist for "SHERO Magazine." She is very active in her community, hosting annual back to school book bag drives, inspirational ladies night out events and assists in serving the less fortunate. She also assists with a Woman's Prison Ministry and is a North Carolina Ambassador for Achotis Under The Talit.

Get to know Author Helen Lawrence:
FB: @helenmlawrence
IG: @Coachladymocha_
Email: mochalive59@gmail.com
Periscope: @Helenmlawrence

Helen Lawrence

Unleashing Sunday Power

Born in Clermont Florida, I grew up living in a normal suburban home. I was blessed to grow up with both of my parents; the late Elder Lonnie Staten Jr. & Catherine Staten. While my rearing was typical, my past is nothing but.

My parents did the best they could with what we had, I never knew any different. They were kind, loving and strong people of faith; active leaders in their local church. We attended church faithfully. We were there for every Tuesday Night Prayer Meeting, which turned into testimony service; every Wednesday Night Bible Study, which turned into an all-out foot stomping, hand clapping, talking in tongues Holy Ghost party; every Thursday Night Deacon Board meeting, followed by choir rehearsal. We didn't even take Fridays off, as we were right back for Friday Night Tarry Service with everyone laying out, prostrate around the altar.

On Sunday morning, I can remember waking up early, around 5am, to the sound of my father singing, *Oh, When Sunday Comes,* while walking through the house, as he started family prayer. The aroma of momma's homemade biscuits with freshly churned butter and homemade preserves from her private food pantry filled the air. I can recall the smell of thick cut bacon still on the rind frying up in a big black cast iron skillet. And of course, there was daddy's hot buttered grits and fresh eggs from the chicken coop. Just the thought of it has my mouth watering and ready for a real down-home southern cooked breakfast.

After breakfast, we were off to 9am Sunday School and 11am church service. We usually ate at the annex but sometimes we went home for Sunday dinner; then back again for 7pm evening church service. Does anyone remember the fifth Sunday meetings, I sure do! I am sure you know what I am talking about, we didn't have a choice back then, everyone went to church! But I'm so thankful for that on today. I am the woman I am today because of it. Back then church wasn't just somewhere to go, it was who we were. Yes, I'm an original PK (Preacher's Kid), and as a PK I knew my parents had my best interest at heart. I may not have understood or agreed with everything my parents said or did, but I was always taught to *acknowledge God in all thy ways and He will direct your path.* (Proverbs: 3:6). My father would always say, "child get yourself somewhere and get quiet, listen for God's voice". Then, "everywhere you go and everything you set out to do, keep God first and He will keep you on the right path." I can hear both of my parents saying, "go to God in prayer child and be sober and vigilant because the adversary (the devil) comes in many shapes, forms and fashions". As I grew up, this helped me to understand that the enemy's plan is always to kill, steal and destroy. As I matured and deepened my understanding of God's Word, my parents' teachings reminded me of Proverb: 22:6-*train up a child in the way he should go and even when he is old he/she will not depart from it.* But I realized that God granted us free will, He also gave us the knowledge to know right from wrong. He gave us the ability to choose which Master to follow and the power to stand strong and fight for what we truly believed in our hearts.

I remember sitting with my mother and talking about life and my going out into the world. She taught me to always protect and respect my Brown Sugar. Hold up, wait a minute, stop! Let me explain about my Brown Sugar. It's definitely more than what you think it is. It's my value and self-worth; my confidence and self-esteem. It's the substance that manifests my belief in myself and those I love and care about. It is the true essence of who I am and defines the authentic me that was purposefully designed by the Creator. It is the precious entity that is my soul; the wholeness, the complete me. Mother's talks taught me that there is a process to mastering the Art of Becoming. It requires us to embrace life's lessons and understand the Art of Release.

After I graduated from high school, I decided to go out on my own, get a job and find an apartment in Orlando. I enrolled at Valencia College and majored in business and customer service. I worked as an assistant office administrator and librarian by day and part-time waitress at night to support myself while in school. Life seemed to be moving in the right direction, but as always, just as soon as things start working in our favor the enemy seems to rear his ugly head. Remember, his plan is always to kill, steal and destroy all that is good and righteous.

One Friday morning, my cousins and a few girl friends came to visit me. We had all graduated from high school together, found good jobs or started college and moved out on our own. So now it was time to all come together again and celebrate our independence. We decided to go out for a lady's night on the town. We had been looking forward to this all week. One of my girlfriends managed a luxury spa in Daytona Beach where they pampered us from head to toe. We even sat in the sauna so our dresses would fit like a sleeve. We got full body massages, facials, fresh hairstyles, nails, and makeup; the full package. After a light lunch and an intense shopping spree, we all went back to my girlfriend's townhouse for a good nap. Later that afternoon it was time for us all to dress for the evening. I slipped on my little black dress and my black stilettos and red accessories.

We were all dressed to kill for a night out on the town. We girls were... On Fire!! We drove to the club and pulled up to the valet five deep in my little Toyota Corolla.

Inside we met up with another relative and his friends. This city would never be the same after tonight! We were looking forward to a night full of fun, family, food, and drinks. Let's get this party started! So, after a few dances, laughs, drinks, and hors d'oeuvres, we were taking our seats and looked up to see another close friend approaching our table. He was one of two twin brothers who we all grew up with from early childhood and he always wore really nice sweaters and denim. The party just went to the next level. We didn't think he was going to make it so everyone was really excited to see him. He was always full of joy and happiness and kept us all rolling with laughter; he was truly the life of the party.

As the night went on with a few more runs to the dance floor, drinks, laughs and hot wings, we were joined by a few more friends and family members that included the other twin brother. This brother was the streetwise hustler and gambler of the two and always wore these sharp leather coats; that's how we could always tell them apart. So now our small group of girls has grown into a large group of very close friends and family with two tables butted together; partying like it was 1999!!

By now the club was packed and pumping and we were all having the best night of our lives. With all the dancing, drinking, and laughing, things were literally starting to heat up inside the club, so some of us decided to step outside for a breath of fresh air. We stood up and the first twin asked to borrow his brother's leather coat to wear outside knowing the night had grown pretty cool and airy.

He put on the coat and grabbed my hand as we all linked hands so we weren't separated moving through the crowd in single file towards the door, still jamming to the beat of the music. As we made it to the door, I felt one of my stiletto heels break. Right as my friend stepped outside the door, I bent down to take my shoe off. All of a sudden, I felt something wet and sticky fall on top of me. My first thought was, "who the heck spilled their drink all over me?" Now I'm boiling mad and being as short as I am, I couldn't see anything through the crowd.

Suddenly, I'm being pushed and shoved and everyone is screaming, ducking, running and scrambling, "Shots fired, get down, get down, shots fired", was all I heard!! At this point I found myself outside the door, still holding on to the twin brother's hand, but the rest of our group was nowhere to be seen. As I turned towards the twin brother to ask what was happening, I was frozen in horror as I realized it wasn't a spilled drink I felt all over my face, hair, and clothes. It was my friend's blood and brain matter, as he slowly fell back on me, still holding my hand. I was in such shock I didn't know if some of the blood was my own or not. Was I shot too? Was I going to die? As he fell back on me like a ton of bricks, the momentum took us both to the ground and now he was lying on top of me bleeding and dying.

As I lay in horror and shock, I remember faintly hearing voices through the cloud of chaos around me asking; "Peaches, can you hear me, can you move, are you okay, are you shot, can you feel anything?" Then I could hear, "stay down, don't move, help is on the way, someone straighten out her leg, no don't touch her, help is coming, there is so much blood, move him off her, no don't touch them, help is on the way". Then I remember thinking, "I still have years ahead of me. Sweet Baby Jesus, I know I'm not perfect but I've tried to live life the best way I know how. I know I haven't dotted every "I", or crossed every "T", but I've tried to treat people the way I wanted to be treated". That's what I was taught by my parents and it's one of the principles in the "Brown Sugar" Code of Ethics. A flood of thoughts raced through my mind, my life flashed before me, then total quiet, then nothing; I lost consciousness. I remember waking up the next morning in the hospital; still traumatized, confused and in shock.

My friends and family were all there around me; some crying tears of joy, some shouting, some were even praying for me. The good news was, I was only grazed by the bullet but suffered a concussion from the fall. My friends told me that because I'm only

4 feet 11 inches tall, my short height was the reason I was still alive. I gave a big sigh and gave God thanks under my breath. The reality was, it was God's Grace and Mercy that had spared my life. Bending down to take off my broken stiletto saved me!

Then came the horrific news. After attempting to get myself together, my next words were; "where is he, how is he, did he make it, what happened??" There was a bone chilling silence in the room, as if time had literally stood still at that moment. The look on their faces and the tears welling up in their eyes told the story; I had my answer. Later I was told my friend died instantly and the bullets he took were really meant for his twin brother who actually owned the leather coat he was wearing.

No one could possibly imagine the deep loss, the fog, the anger, the unbearable pain and hurt I felt. I couldn't seem to wrap my head around it or understand who could do this to us; to my friend. He had also just started to branch out and develop his career as an uprising realtor. I couldn't seem to pull myself together and my friends and family had no answers.

Every question I asked, nobody knew anything. The police investigation was ongoing, so we were being told very little about the progress. I remained hospitalized through the night for observation due to the concussion. Everyone was really worried about me because I couldn't seem to stay focused. I had nightmares, night sweats, no appetite, insomnia, memory loss and experienced anxiety attacks. I was told by the doctors that this would go on for several weeks or more but it would pass. I wasn't released to go back to work for months. I felt sick to my stomach and at times, the pain was so overwhelming. One minute I was okay; the next, I felt lost and alone.

Now the time was approaching to attend the funeral service of my friend. My girlfriends picked me up to attend the service. I remember feeling nothing; absolutely nothing. I was completely numb.

As I sat through the service, the tears rolled down my face; I was completely shattered and broken inside. I never got the chance to tell him how much I loved him or that I was so proud of him. I never got the chance to say a final goodbye. I was devastated even though I knew the Creator makes no mistakes. He is the giver and taker of all life in His infinite wisdom and timing; but I never got a chance to say a final goodbye.

When I found out the wrong twin brother was killed and the shooters identified him by his brother's leather coat, the discovery made it all so much worse. I hated his brother for that and a million question rang in my head: "Why did he let his brother wear his coat? Why didn't he come outside with us? Did he know that this a setup? Were they after me?"

When I voiced these questions in my head, I felt like life had kicked me right in my chest and snatched my breath away. My life started spiraling downward and I went into a deep depression. I was fearful, unhappy and didn't want to be around anyone. I didn't want to talk to anyone and didn't accept phone calls, not even from my parents. I literally closed the doors and cut everyone out of my life while I drowned in grief... But I never got to say a final goodbye.

After about three weeks of total seclusion, there was a knock on my door early one Sunday morning. When I didn't answer, the lock turned and the door opened. To my surprise, it was my father to whom I had given a key for emergency situations.

He looked at me and said, *"Get up from there, daughter. Don't you know that because of Him, death has no sting, the grave no victory? You child, can start again, and again and again. Now, "When Sunday Comes," you don't have to cry no more. "When Sunday Comes," trouble gone and Jesus will soothe your troubled mind. Leave all your heart aches behind. Get yourself up from there daughter and gather some things, your mama sent me to fetch you home for a while."*

So, I gathered my things, we jumped in his Buick and we started on the trip home. It seemed like the longest ride of my life, we didn't say much but he just kept singing; "When Sunday Comes," troubles gone.

Later that night, I was home in my old room, lying in my old bed, crying my eyes out. I had awakened startled from another nightmare; I was reliving that night in my mind over and over again. I looked over at my old prayer chair sitting in the corner of the room and my mother was sitting there in the dark, quietly praying the Lord's Prayer. She never even opened her eyes but she said,

"Quiet yourself child. I know you're hurting and confused right now, but you're safe at home now. Now get yourself up and get in posture".

At that very moment, my father walked into the room and anointed my head with oil, then he kneeled down beside me. Then my mother said, "Now, ask God to grant you the serenity to accept the things you cannot change, and the courage to change the things that you can, and the wisdom to know the difference. Ask Him to help you live one day at a time, to experience joy one moment at a time. Accepting hardship as the pathway to peace, taking as He did, this sinful world as it is, and not as you would have it to be. But learning to trust that He will make all things right when you surrender to His will. That you may be reasonably happy in this life and supremely happy with Him forever in the next."

Both my mother and father got up, kissed me on my forehead like I was still their little girl and left the room. My soul began to cry out and the tears began to flow.

"LORD, I NEED YOU TO HELP ME!!" So, I stepped up to the dresser mirror and took a good long look at myself. Not just the me, in the mirror, but the inner me. I asked myself this question, because sometimes you just got to have a conversation with yourself, woman to woman. I looked in the mirror and spoke:

HOW THE HECK DID WE GET HERE? Yes girl, I know that you're overwhelmed, filled with grief and I know you want to just throw in the towel. I see you at the brink of giving up and ending it all, but now it's time to encourage yourself. Yes, it did happen, and yes it happened to you. There's a void; a big hurt, a heaviness, disappointment and uncertainty. But GOD!!! RELEASE IT ALL!!! Now BREATHE, inhale-exhale; now pick yourself up out of this pit of depression and get your life back, BREATHE AGAIN DEEPLY, inhale-exhale; steady your feet on solid ground and live your life.

I had to remind myself that I am not my past and I couldn't allow this tragic moment to define the rest of my life! I had to get up and get myself together. I had to realize that there was nothing I could have done and it wasn't my fault. I had to forgive. No matter what you are going through, you must give yourself permission to forgive you. You can't hold on to anger, hurt or pain. These things steal your growth, energy, strength and power.

As you face tragedies, remember the Brown Sugar Code of Ethics – the necessary strength, courage, and wisdom, to overcome is already in you, just tap into it! Your inner strength drives you and sustains you. That same strength carries your spirit, your being, your self-worth and your self-esteem. Always remember that you are of a Royal Priesthood, a Queen, a Lioness, a Warrior, a Survivor, a Daughter of Jerusalem and a Conqueror. You are Fearfully and Wonderfully made in God's image.

<u>What I Have Learned: Wisdom From A SHERO</u>

- When Sunday Comes- Is the very second that you come to yourself and the light bulb comes on in the heart and spirit of your mind, enlightenment, the epiphany, Hello!! The reality of walking into your breakthrough, a place where you are no longer stuck or bound and the chains are broken. God has been there the whole time waiting on you to recognize the great and awesome power of His true anointing lying deep within you.

- Never Quit - You may pause for a Reset, Reboot, New Beginning but never give up! There is a difference between giving up and knowing when enough is enough. Release it, dump all the negativity, hurt and pain in your life. Forgive yourself and them and move on. Start Over and Launch a New and Fresh anointing for your life.

- Love who God has Designed you to be - It's all for His Glory and His Purpose for your life. Allow Him into your life and evolve from a mere caterpillar into a Beautiful, Powerful & Passionate Butterfly on your way to your Destiny!

Author Kim Wilson

Kim Wilson is a 29-year-old resident of Elizabeth City, NC. Kim is a Youth Motivational Speaker, Licensed Substance Abuse Therapist, Behavior Specialist, Certified Youth Mental Health First Aid Instructor, Infant Toddler Family Specialist, and a Certified Life Coach. Kim's work experience is in many fields, which attests to her strong work ethic. She makes it her priority to set positive examples for the younger generation. Giving back to the community has always been a goal in her life.

She has experienced many challenges in her life that led her to start Girls for Empowerment. Girls for Empowerment is a 501c3 organization serving girls, ages 5-18, focusing on Character Building, Education Enhancement, Community Service, and Cultural and Self Awareness, all while providing participants with the necessary skills to navigate through life obstacles. The organization hosts monthly community service events ranging from: interactions with the elderly, volunteering at agencies and schools, toy and food drives, and highway clean-up activities.

Despite her challenges, Kim has made a good life for herself, her daughters and youth in the community. She has observed many young girls make bad life decisions, which resulted in teen-age pregnancies, low self-esteem, poor judgment, imprisonment (detention center), high school drop-outs, and life dropouts. As a result, Kim was motivated to reach out to other counties to start a Girls for Empowerment Club in their areas.

Kim prays Girls for Empowerment organization will establish a firm foundation that will allow young girls to be themselves and seek help if needed and make good decisions in achieving their goals. Kim has facilitated many support groups for youth and families, ranging from suicide awareness and prevention, R. E. A. D. (Reading Everyday Advances Development), Youth Leadership Training: Prevention Plus Wellness, Bullying Awareness and Prevention, Self-Esteem and Self-Love. Kim believes that it does take a VILLAGE to raise a child so it is very important for everyone to come together and help make this organization successful in reaching out to every youth. She is very hard working and gives selflessly to those who are in need. Her priority is making sure the youth in the community have a positive place where they are comfortable, able to FREELY express themselves, and intertwine with who they are. Kim's passion for the youth and her community is very strong and positive.

Get to know Author Kim Wilson:
girlsforempowerment@gmail.com
252-312-0516
www.girlsforempowerment.com

Kim Wilson

Unleashing The Self Love

"The purest and most genuine form of love is Self-Love"

We face challenges daily. Out of all the challenges we face, battling your identity, self-worth and self-esteem are some of the important ones. When you lack high self-esteem, you tend to be more vulnerable and easily accessible. Self-Esteem is how you feel about yourself. Often, we allow society to dictate who we are internally and externally. We allow social media to determine how we see ourselves. We look at the women in the videos, magazines, movies, and news and attempt to transform our mind and body to imitate their appearance and lifestyle. In doing so, we lose our sense of self and fall victim to society's dream and image. We become just another woman living in their world instead of "our" world.

What is love? That's a question that is often asked numerous times by a woman who has experienced a bad relationship with a man whom she thought of as the love of her life. Love can become so complex; so confusing. It can have you thinking things are authentic and genuine when it can be far from the reality. I truly believe it is impossible to love someone or to receive love from others, if there's a lack of self-love.

On September 5, 1987, a "small chocolate" baby was born into the world. I was the middle child and the darkest in the family. As a child, I loved watching Nickelodeon and I loved reading and writing. I grew up in a house where there were a variety of things going on, ranging from sibling rivalry to isolation.

My mother was a mother who worked multiple jobs to take care of the children and the house. My mother labored not for herself, but for her children. My mom felt that she displayed "love", to me and my siblings, through the provisions and security that she provided. There were few times when the family ate dinner at the table together. Everyone was usually in their own space and there was little to no communication.

Affection was not readily shown. To the best of her ability and knowledge, she did show love. I remember getting a few hugs from my mom. My father was absent: as he stayed in and out of jail throughout my life. Growing up without a father, I never knew what a father's love felt like. The few memories I had of my father were not pleasant; they were not examples of love.

Often, I felt like the "outcast" of the family. I was the darkest of the family. I experienced being bullied and being called, "black attack" and other derogatory names because of my dark complexion. I began to dislike my own skin. Throughout my childhood and adolescence, as I watched movies and videos, looked in the newspaper, and observed my classmates in relationships; it was always girls of lighter complexion who seemed to have everything in order and were successful and happy. I often wondered what my life would be like if I was a little lighter. My self-esteem was extremely low. I was slowly, but surely losing myself.

I tried to become part of the "in crowd" in high school. I wanted to be popular and have friends and get noticed. However, I encountered so many bad friendships with females that I felt I no longer understood the definition of friendship. The females I considered friends revealed, through their behavior towards me, that they were not my friends. They were very manipulative and often engaged in risky behaviors. There was no uplifting or encouragement; only fights and arguments. Peer pressure was a very prevalent and serious for me.

During my high school years, I was in one committed relationship for about 2 ½ years that ended abruptly without an explanation. I was devastated and did not understand what caused the relationship to end. I questioned whether I was the cause of the break up. Had I done something wrong? Was I not good enough for him? So many thoughts and questions went through my mind; to which I had no answers.

When I attended college, I met new people and had so much fun. However, without having proper knowledge of a "real" relationship, I pretty much jumped head first into my first college relationship. After a few dates, I was head- over- hills in love with him; only to find out I wasn't the only woman in his life. When I realized that he was telling me and the other woman the same blatant lies, I ended the relationship. Honestly, I did not end the relationship because I wanted to, but rather because I was afraid of what others were going to say about me for staying and sharing him. Although this relationship was fairly short, I had already given him money, and even washed his clothes, thinking that was the way to keep and make a man happy. There were other relationships but they were not successful or healthy.

Fortunately, during my college years, I met two young ladies who were the true definition of a "friend" and when I was with them, I felt I did not have to be someone else; I could be myself. Even though I thought I exhibited the traits that I wanted in a friend, there were periods when I didn't. Being honest, I had to admit that I couldn't expect something from someone if I didn't model the standard that I was expecting from them. To have a friend, you must first, be a friend.

After those relationship experiences, I refocused on my completing college. I graduated with a degree in Psychology and was successful in finding a job I loved. I had always dreamed of the man of my life. It wasn't until 2011 that I resumed dating. I met a special man and after three years of being in a strong relationship, we were blessed with the birth of our daughter.

March of this year-2017, this special man proposed and we are currently planning a wedding. Reflecting on past relationships, I realized I had allowed myself to be used and mentally abused by all the men I previously encountered. No more! I realized "enough was enough". I also realized no one was going to treat me the way I wanted to be treated if I didn't demand it. I experienced all those bad relationships with men because I had no knowledge of what to look for in an intimate relationship. I had no idea how to love or receive love from a man. I was not sexually active with all the men I dated; however, I allowed my heart to get broken numerous times. I had no idea that to receive and give love I had to first, love myself unconditionally; including my imperfect flaws.

I accepted who I was. I gained a better understanding of the beauty of my dark complexion. I learned to love me just the way I am. Once I began doing that, my self-esteem increased and whenever people said or did something negative to me, it didn't bother me because my character was so much stronger than before.

I no longer cared what people thought of me. My sanity was more important and my girls needed me more than anything. I had to live my life for me! **I had to Unleash Self-love!**

What I Have Learned: Wisdom From A SHERO

1. During those trying obstacles of my past, I lost sense of self. I had to meditate and discover myself again. I discovered that Self-Identity is very important to your success. Self-identity is the recognition of your potential and qualities as an individual. Once you become aware of who you are, then you can make positive choices in life; you are able to be a part of the "out" crowd rather than the "in" crowd. You can say "no", and not be easy prey to negative peer pressure. You can love yourself first before seeking love from others.

2. Your family, their history, and environment also play a major part in you determining who you are. Contrary to belief, you have the power to not allow your environment or history to determine the true you. It is normal to use those things as processing tools to assist you in identifying who you are. Self-discovery brings peace within. It allows you to look deeper within to unlock those hidden talents and traits. I consider Self-actualization as one of the highest human needs.

3. You are an individual with your own uniqueness and creativity. Knowing and understanding who you are increases more opportunities for success. You will then be able to know your dreams and goals and develop steps to accomplish them. You will be able to interact with others without doubt or shame because through it all you are being "you". When you love yourself without limits you can love others and allow others to love you.

4. Until I became in tune with myself and had a sense of self, I struggled with pleasing others and living my life for others. Even though I could set goals and develop a plan to accomplish those goals I still doubted my abilities, questioned my actions, and was overly concerned about how people would respond. It was then, that I realized I didn't have a real idea of "self-knowledge". Awareness of self brings you an aurora of positivity that not only

impacts your life but impacts the lives of others around you. Understanding who you are is a major factor in making positive choices. Making positive choices is essential to the soul and the development of a successful, healthy, competent woman.

5. Making choices sometimes means you will make the wrong choices to get to the right choices. In my life, I made choices that were wrong but I turned those wrong choices into something positive. Often, we lose sense of self by living up to others' expectations, beliefs, and desires. We must be able to recognize our worth and demand respect. You must take the time to genuinely define who you are internally. There are so many misconceptions of who society, family, and environment say we are that we become unsure.

6. Strength and Power; the two things you will need to start redirecting your path and focusing on self. Focus on the things that will help you unleash the positive characteristic traits of "you". If you don't know who you are, then how do you expect for others to know. Tell yourself positive things every morning. When you do, you will believe, and soon after, the love for yourself will increase. There's a scripture in the bible that reads "speak those things as if they were" …Self Love is essential! Don't' beat yourself up over the past…move forward. Take at least one hour for yourself daily (read, write, eat dinner, shop, clean, rest). Don't lose yourself trying to make others happy and pleased. Recognize that you hold the key to your own happiness. Prepare yourself for greatness. Recognize you are a precious jewel waiting to shine; to shine you must first realize the purest form of love is self-love.

7. It is essential to be a leader that is striving to make a change in the community. In order to see change, you must be the change and seek out to recruit leaders like yourself. "Change it starts with you!"

You Are...

You are beautiful
You are strong
You are determined
You are courageous
You are a leader
You are nice
You are a helper
You are a mother
You are smart
You are a WOMAN!
You are somebody...You are "YOU"

Author Sharonette Smart

Sharonette Smart was born in April of 1969, in Savannah, Ga. She says her greatest accomplishments are her four beautiful daughters, Zachoyia, Ciara, Amiya, and Shaniya.

Sharonette is the Founder and CEO of Single Mothers United of the World, Inc., a Non-profit Organization that supports single moms and their children. She is a Domestic Engineer (Formerly Known as Single Mother), Evangelist, Entrepreneur, Impartation Messenger, Real Estate Broker, Life Insurance Producer, Founder and CEO of SmartChoice Publishing Group, LLC, and SISter!

Her passion for her call to serve others, has fueled her purpose, and driven her assignment to break the stigmas that are placed on the lives of single mothers. As a Domestic Engineer (Formerly Known as Single Mother) for 26 years, Ms. Smart has endured tests, trials, and tribulations that have shaped and molded her into the phenomenal woman she is today.

Sharonette's book, "The Load I Carry...Cast Your Cares! ~ A 31 Day Inspiration Devotional" is dedicated to Single Moms (or Domestic Engineers), and was birthed out of her process and journey. She wanted to provide other Domestic Engineers with a resource that would encourage, empower, and inspire them to Live in Purpose! To never give up; and to never give in. To encourage them to trust God even when they can't feel Him; to just know He's there. Her motto is...

"I Am My Sister's Keeper! Together We Are Stronger!"

"We Are More Powerful Together Than We Will Ever Be Apart!"

Sharonette Smart

Unleashing The Side Chick Mindset

W hy am I so comfortable lying here in the arms of another woman's husband, her man, after making passionate love to him with no restraints. Loving and living life as if I'm the wife, knowing good and well, that when morning comes he'll leave my arms for hers. When did this become acceptable, this mindset, that what we are doing is okay? When did it develop? Was it the fact that I was born to teenage parents; so the cards were already stacked against me. Or that daddy left mommy when I was 18 months old. Or was it the rape that occurred when I was 7 years old? Perhaps it was the loss of my virginity at the age of 14 years old, or my leaving home at 14 years old, having to survive by any means necessary. I'm not sure which event or the combination thereof, formed this mindset in me. All I know is, it took place early in my life, and it took on an identity of its own. This "Side Chick Mindset" would go on to mold my very existence.

I was 14, grown, and on my own, or so I thought. I was beautiful, fine, and operated heavily in the power of persuasion, also known as manipulation, also known as witchcraft. These attributes gave the enemy all the ammunition he needed to use against me. Sadly, I would ultimately become my own worst enemy. After being raped at the age of 7, I had no idea that a spiritual portal had been opened in my life to sexual perversion, and immorality. It would however, lie dormant until around the age of twelve, when some family members, friends, and I (all girls), began to explore the pleasures of one another. (This opened me up to another issue that we won't cover in this chapter.) Then, when I consented to having sex for the first time at the age of 14, I fully unlocked and released the sexual demon that had laid dormant in me for many years. I can remember equating sex to love and love to sex. That was a warped mindset, but I was a hungry 14-year-old girl, looking for love, so I had a whole lot of sex, because it was my love language. Love was what I craved; believing it would fill the void. Like with any addiction, it controlled my life, and the older I got, the worst it got;

this mindset of mine. The void grew larger. No matter how many relationships I invaded or families I destroyed; I was still empty.

I was always attracted to older men. I'd later learn that it was a symptom of the "Absentee Daddy" syndrome. As a result, most of the men I encountered were old enough to be my daddy. Nine times out of ten, they were someone else's daddy, or either someone else's husband, or boyfriend. You see, leaving home at the ripe age of 14, left me vulnerable to the enemy's devices; I was uncovered. I had always been the Side Chick, Side Piece, Side Kick, or the Clean- Up Woman. This position, posture, and mindset became a safe place for me to camp out in. Although it was biblically and morally wrong, it kept me secure and in control. I said- who, what, when, and where. It seemed that I held all the cards, but you see that's the thing about sin; it beguiles and deceives. It takes you further than you want to go and keeps you longer than you planned to stay. I lived like this seemingly all my life. Repeatedly falling in lust, because I had no true definition of what love really was. My mom did the best she could with what she had. I later learned that her definition of love handicapped her too. Just in a different way. So, it would seem the spiritual deficiency that gripped me at the core had a source; a bloodline. Often, we can trace various traits in our lives to sources within our family; our bloodline. For instance, I observed that the men on both sides; maternal and paternal, had an appetite that one woman couldn't satisfy. This spirit didn't have a gender preference when it came to the generations that followed, because I think the females were just as bad, if not worse than the males. Just my opinion.

As I reflect on my life; the events that took place, the relationships I had, and the transitions throughout my life, I thank God that my journey, my process, took place within the timeframe that it did. I say this because today's version of the Side Chick is so vastly different from what I experienced. Perhaps it's because, unlike my Queen Sisters of today, (who by the way, just haven't yet come to the revelation that they are a Queen), I clearly understood my position and it was never necessary for me to operate outside of those agreed upon parameters. What do I mean? Glad you asked. A true Side Chick, Side Piece, Side Kick, or Clean- Up Woman, knows her place; her position, and if she is truly good at it, she can flow in an atmosphere occupied by the wife or girlfriend undetected and unassuming. This is because her position is understood; there is no need for a "flag on the play" when the key players know the rules. What I see today is a lot of young ladies, who lack a sense of value just like I did, but they also lack discretion and class. If you have chosen to take on the position of a Side Chick, then assume it! There is absolutely no need for you to advertise to the world or promote the fact that you lack value and morals. Ultimately that's what we are saying when we advertise, promote, and draw attention to our mess. Notice, I said we! You see, I came to God just as I was; a hot mess, Side Chick, and all. Heck, I'm STILL a work in progress. I made no excuses, and I couldn't hide who I was from Him. Yet, He chose me, despite my bad choices in life. God had a plan to use me. I wasn't immediately delivered from this warped mindset. Did you hear me? Yes, you! The one reading my chapter! I was in God, in church, and I still struggled with the mindset. I still assumed the position. I used to wonder how God could use me;

how He could still love me, when I couldn't seem to kick this habit, this struggle, this mindset. Yet, God continued to extend grace and mercy to me. I could have written about anything, there is enough Word and Wisdom in me that I could have written a chapter with five points and a close, but I felt it was important for me to expose the devil since he figures he's going to glorify this warped mindset and spiritual deficiency with a reality show. As a society, as a human race, we have lost our moral compass. It's bad enough that there are women and men, who for whatever reason, are willing to compromise the sanctity of their marriage, but it's a whole different planet on which we operate, if we are willing to glorify it with a reality TV show. We must expose the devil for who he really is. Being a Side Chick or having the mindset of one is a direct result of a spiritual deficiency that has invaded the lives and mindsets of those assuming the position. Yet, before we can judge the journey we must understand the process. You don't have to put yourself in the shoes of a Side Chick, to understand her or him, because there is no gender discrimination. If the truth be told, becoming a Side Chick can be as unassuming as entertaining a conversation with a co-worker, attending a lunch you were invited to by a church member, or coffee at Starbuck's with your Pastor. Oh, ya'll didn't know, Pastors have Side Chicks too. Okay, since you're reading my chapter judging me, let me expose you to the mindset. Sex is sex! But INTIMACY is a whole different playing field. You see the issue is not your man having sex with another woman; the issue is your man connecting INTIMATELY with another woman. She has tapped into a deficiency within him through intimate knowledge and conversations and now he wants more stimulation. Now let's be clear, since there is no gender discrimination in the term Side Chick. There are just as many women as there are men, who are also stepping outside marriage or committed relationships and cavorting with their Side Piece. Men and women alike, must take ownership of the role they play in this warped game and evil web, because it impacts too many innocent lives.

You see, when I was endorsing this role I never considered the other players, the wife, the kids, the family. It was never my concern. I never considered the pain and destruction my role of

Side Chick would cause if it was ever uncovered, or exposed. That is, not until my role was reversed and I became the wife. Even as a young woman, I always knew that one day I would reap the seeds I had sown. The pain I had caused others would one day come searching for me, and it did. When I got married back in 1999, I knew that I wasn't going to live happily ever after; because the young people of today say- I had too many "bodies". I had destroyed too many marriages and relationships for me to think my marriage was going to survive. If the truth be told, as I was walking down the aisle to get married, I heard the Spirit of God say, "Turn and run now, they will talk now, but you won't cry later". My photographer actually caught that very moment in a photograph as I was coming down the aisle, in conversation with the Spirit of God. I shared this because retribution is real! Early in my marriage, I thought I was doing everything right; everything I was supposed to·do. I thought I had inside knowledge, having experienced the other side as the Side Chick. Yet, Side Chicks still impacted my marriage. I found myself following up on a rumor and confronting one of the women. However, the fate of my marriage would be determined by my own first cousin. Yes, two brothers' children; we had the same blood running through our veins. This was a devastating betrayal! This Side Chick invasion was supposed to kill me, but when the smoke cleared and the pain subsided, God ministered to me and let me know, this too shall pass. Through the pain, He coached me to develop compassion and empathy. As a result, I understood the pain I had caused others. This gave me the courage to reach back and ask for forgiveness from several of the women I had hurt. I never understood the pain I caused others, until I experienced it for myself. I didn't write this chapter to glorify my actions, but to expose them so that someone else who has found themselves in a similar situation can know that there is hope. Whether you're the Side Chick or the wife; there is purpose for our process and God will not put any more on us than we can bear. So, if you find yourself on either side know that God is a restorer, a healer, and a deliverer. He can and will make your crooked places straight. I'm not bitter I'm better! Better because I didn't die in what was designed to kill me, and neither will you. I was transformed by the renewing of my mind.

Romans 12:2 When God chose me, He knew what He was getting. Yet, He chose me. He has chosen you too; be free my Queen Sister, be free! *Let this mind be in you which was also in Christ Jesus.* **Philippians 2:5**

What I Have Learned: Wisdom From A SHERO

- A Side Chick Mindset is a direct result of a Spiritual Deficiency; a lack of self-worth and value.

- You can't judge an individual's process without understanding their journey.

- You will never be The Wife, no matter how many lies he tells you. If he leaves his family for you, he'll soon leave you for a newer model.

- It was the love of God that apprehended me, that rescued me from a path and life of destruction. Let Him free you too. Refuse to be a Side Chick any longer!

SIS, LOVE YOURSELF BETTER THAN THAT!" "GET YOUR LIFE BACK!"

Sharonette Smart, DE

You Have The
Power To
Unleash Your SHERO

Author Sheresa Elliot

Sheresa Elliot was born to Melvin Elliot Sr. and late Machel Vaughan on July 11, 1988. She was born in Williamston, NC and raised in Bertie County, NC the beginning of her life. She has one older sibling, Melvin Elliot Jr. and a younger adoptive sister, Monasha Barnes. Sheresa attended Riverview Elementary in Murfreesboro, NC and graduated from Hertford County High School in 2006.

While in high school, at the age of 16, Sheresa developed a love for social work. Her parents were called to care for some children that were physically abused. Witnessing their love and support for these children in need, sparked Sheresa's interest. Sheresa was fascinated by the social worker, who performed their home visits; checking for safety and quality care. Sheresa always had a love for serving and helping those in difficult situations. From that home visit, Sheresa knew that she wanted to pursue social work.

Sheresa attended Winston Salem State University located in Winston-Salem, NC. Upon graduation from WSSU, Sheresa began her career in Social Work with Northampton County Department of Social Services. She was employed as a Work First Social Worker where she assisted individuals with tools and resources to secure employment. Sheresa was a diligent worker and succeeded through all the challenges. Sheresa is currently employed with Carteret County Social Services as a Foster Care Licensing Worker.

In this job role, Sheresa recruits foster parents and provides them with a state required training call MAPP (Model Approach to Partnership in Parent). Highly trained and experienced, she is certified to teach this specialized course anywhere in the U.S. She completes the application process for all families interested in fostering or adoption. Sheresa enjoys her current position as she dreamed to work with the Child Protective Services department. Sheresa is currently a Masters of Social Work student at East Carolina University. She is on track to graduate with a MSW May 2018.

Sheresa is also the founder of *I Am Her, INC*. I Am Her, INC., is a nonprofit organization established to empower, motivate and prepare females ages 13-18 for young adulthood. The program is based out of Hertford County, NC as Sheresa travels to different locations to inspire youth. This program focuses on self-esteem and self-confidence, health and nutrition, decision-making skills and proper etiquette just to name a few. Sheresa enjoys using her personal experiences to motivate youth and inspiring them to invest in their future. Sheresa also has a personal brand, *I Am Sheresa*, where she serves as a Confidence and Personal Development Coach.

Get to know Author Sheresa Elliot:

iamsheresaelliot@gmail.com

www.iamherinc.com

FB: I Am Her Inc. & I Am Sheresa

Sheresa Elliot

Unleashing The Unspoken

"You are going to college."

"You will not sit around here and not make something of yourself."

"High school is not your final stop."

All of these things were said to me as a senior in high school. I did not expect college would be easy. I knew there would be challenges, hardships, and obstacles. I knew my parents would not be with me every single day to hold my hand and I would now have to hold myself accountable.

I felt like I had it altogether. I was offered an opportunity to work in the Career Services Office for work study. I submitted all my assignments timely. I arrived to class on time, but I was also home sick. I longed for my family and couldn't shake the isolation of college. To solve this, I traveled home every single weekend to find comfort. As I increased my travel, I started to miss classes and exams. Then it happened. Yes, the thing that happens to about

25% of college students. As a result of failing two courses and missing a final exam my freshman semester, I ended up on academic probation. My GPA dropped to a 1.8!!

I felt an array of emotions. I was devastated. I was embarrassed. I was distraught. I felt like my college career had instantly ended. I worried and stressed constantly about what people would think of me. I worried about what my parents would say. I lied to my friends and told them I did not get housing because I ended up in the dorm without air conditioning. I was ashamed! I felt less than. This was not the child my parents raised me to be! I had to come up with plan—QUICK!

I was given a lot of advice and tips about campus safety, safe sex and watching my surroundings while attending college parties. I, however, was not given advice about how to bounce back from a failure. No one told me once you hit rock bottom you have to work ten times harder to get ahead. No one even told me it was possible! What "they" actually told me was once your GPA dropped below a 2.0 you will never be able to get it back up. Let's just say I aimed to prove "them" wrong. I was determined to graduate-on time with at least a 3.0.

Each and every single day was a battle. I did not have any room for mistakes. I could not miss a class. I could not skip an assignment. This required social and personal sacrifice. I had to miss some college parties. I had to stay on campus instead of traveling back home on weekends. This was truly challenging for me.

I missed my family and every opportunity I had to be with them I took it. This chapter in my life showed me who I truly was. At 18 years old, I had not done any true self-discovery. I did not know what my strengths were. I did not know where to go for resources. Every single summer until I graduated from Winston Salem State University, I attended summer school. I had to retake courses I failed and make up courses I missed in my curriculum in order to stay on track. I was determined to not allow this obstacle in my life to defeat me. I discovered strength I did not know I had. I discovered power within myself that I did not know existed. I tapped into things that were instilled in me as a child. However, in the midst of this storm I had to start telling myself things that people did not tell me as a growing young adult.

As an adult, what I have discovered to be true is that we are unsure of how to talk to our youth and prepare them for young adulthood. We are afraid of saying too much or keeping it 'too' real. We fail to discuss or mention the qualities an individual needs when they are at what appears to be, in that moment, one of their lowest points in life. We need to know as parents, mentors, grandparents, or family members that it is okay to have real conversations with our youth. Provide the youth with tips or advice they can use when faced with adversity. We have to let them know that it is ok to not always be okay.

What I Have Learned: Wisdom From A SHERO

- *Be Strong*- While going through this process, I heavily relied on three words to get me through: Strong, Courageous and Determined. I pray these words help you overcome adversity, obstacles and difficult life challenges that you may face. People do not tell us to be Strong. They tell us to keep fighting, but they do not teach us HOW to keep fighting. To be strong first means to acknowledge that you are worthy, capable and that you have the strength within you to overcome every obstacle you face. It means to have an understanding of what is required of you to have a positive, everlasting impact on the world. To be strong is to be resilient. Face the obstacle and quickly identify a solution. It is critical for us to know our situation may bend us, but it will not break us. When faced with a challenge, view it as growing pains and an opportunity to learn from those mistakes. When obstacles arise understand that it is simply a moment in time and that it is only temporary. Your dreams and goals are bigger than your challenges. Focus more on the goals and less on your current circumstance.

- *Be Courageous*- People do not tell us to be Courageous. They tell us to not be arrogant and conceited, but they do not teach us to stand up for what we believe in. It is totally okay for people to not understand you and your dreams. After all, it is your dream. Some people will not understand why you grind so hard. If you feel passionate about something, stand up and say so--and do not feel bad about it. Let your voice be heard and your work be seen. The truth is, anyone can do anything for 20 seconds, but a courageous person will consistently work hard towards something that is meant to last forever.

- *Be Determined*- People do not tell us to be Determined. They tell us not to give up, but they do not explain to us what that might cost us. At some point, all determined people make sacrifices. Sometimes daily sacrifices are necessary when you are trying to achieve greatness. A determined person does not give up. They work harder than the average person and do not let resistance win. Resistance will attack a determined person every opportunity it gets. Determined people use their time wisely. They do not misuse or abuse time that is essential for their progress. Determined people ignore distractions and focus solely on activities needed to attain success.

Be strong.

Be Courageous.

Be Determined.

Author Chemeka Williams

Chemeka Williams has been described as a "new and unique voice in the earth." Delivering well-rooted, well-studied messages of inspiration and empowerment, Chemeka gives her audience a fresh perspective. With foundations in skilled advocacy, oratorical abilities, and scholarship, Chemeka infuses her motivational and perspicacious teachings with a sense of history, as well as the contributions of modern thinkers and teachers.

Chemeka is a single mother of four vivacious and purpose-driven children: Tatiyanna, a sophomore at Saint Augustine University in Raleigh, Shaleik, a senior and honor student, Naseyah and Nacyiah, honor students, attending NCCU Early College.

Chemeka has numerous accolades and accomplishments. She received her Associates of IST (Informational Systems and Technology) from Halifax Community College. Bachelors of Arts in Elementary Education from North Carolina Central University, Masters of Arts in Counseling from Cambridge College and her E.D.S (Educational Specialist in School Administration) from Cambridge College.

In 2015, Chemeka launched *Purpose Driven Coaching* and *Pearls of Purpose Mentoring Services,* a worldwide feminist institution for women of all ages. An educator in public and private schools for nine years, Chemeka also served in various roles throughout her community. Chemeka has served as the Town Commissioner of Garysburg, NC, overseeing the Parks & Recreation Department for four years. Chemeka also served on several boards, including the Town of Garysburg CDS, Board of Roanoke Valley Adult Day Center, and Department of Public Safety (DPS) of Women's Correctional Institution. She currently serves as the Executive Administrator for a rising fortune five hundred non-profit, Mandate Enterprise.

Filled with the desire to not only share her story of adversity and success, but to empower people by providing practical information and insight to help them live better lives. Chemeka is an I.C.F. (international Coaching Federation) Certified Life Coach, which makes professional empowerment valid. Drawing from her decades of educational experience, Chemeka offers educative seminars in areas including: estate planning, financial literary, family relational development and health, domestic violence awareness and leadership development.

Her commitment to living a healthy life- mind, body and spirit- led her to assist in the development of a health and wellness program for women. This program provides practical health and wellness information through the teachings of experts in the field.

Chemeka and several business partners facilitate entrepreneurship seminars, throughout the nation, to inform and inspire those who dream of owning their own business. They strive to provide alternatives for establishing and maintaining financial stability in uncertain economic environments. Chemeka's insights in leadership, facilitating your purpose and women's empowerment allowed her to help hundreds of women move from surviving to LIVING LIFE ON PURPOSE.

Get to know Author Chemeka Williams:

Organization- Pearls of Purpose

Chemeka Williams

Unleashing My Broken Pieces

I n the midst of your brokenness, know that your BROKEN PIECES HAVE PURPOSE!!! As you navigate through life, it is impossible to not experience brokenness and pain. Brokenness is not selective to any race, culture, or socioeconomic status. An element that we understand universal is PAIN. Whether it is feeling the pain of a broken promise, experiencing and surviving trauma, experiencing the pain of broken relationships, broken dreams, or dealing with a broken heart, life has a way of allowing us to experience a BREAKING!!

Your heart has now encountered brokenness. You are damaged, you are wounded; it appears that you cannot escape the pain that has attached itself to the breaking that has taken place. You are now dying mentally, emotionally, physically and spiritually because someone has entered in and destroyed the very thing that you need to live. The pain of the brokenness of your past and present is unbearable and you are asking God- "Why ME?"

Why did I have to be molested? Why was my innocence taken? Why did they abuse me? Why did they leave me tattered with scars? Why did my child have to die? Why did my husband abandon me? Why was I forced to be a single parent? Why was my family torn apart? Why am I being rejected? Why won't they love me? Am I not good enough? Why do I have to be homeless? I didn't know my life would be ripped apart with no warning. I never realized the load I carry would be so great!!! I didn't understand that my valuable thing on the inside would cause chaos to surround me. I didn't know that persecution was required to birth promotion! I have too many broken pieces that I am trying to put back together again. I am SCREAMING for HELP from ALL MY BROKENNESS!

God, then must remind you that the very thing that broke you will push you closer to your PURPOSE. The very thing that tried to swallow you up will take you into your destiny! YOUR PURPOSE IS GREATER THAN THE PAIN OF YOUR BROKENNESS!! Your brokenness has a blessing attached to it. The Bible says, "The sufferings of this present time are not worthy to be compared with the glory that shall be revealed in us" (Romans 8:18). When we think about God's Word, it helps us bear some of the things we have gone through and the trials we face now. The broken pieces were a blueprint for your PURPOSE.

Who desires pain? Who desires to be broken? Although none of us want brokenness to define and identify what we may have experienced in our lives, quite often that is the path our journey leads us to. When our hearts are broken, our vision distorted, our lives devastated and uprooted, our dreams turned to grief and pain; we must give it over to God. God wants to mend us and make us whole. He desires to heal us totally from our past and the pain that we have encountered. There is no pain too great that God cannot heal it. He heals the broken-hearted, and binds up their wounds.

You may ask "What is my purpose?" Your purpose is the very reason for your existence. It is what you were placed on this earth to do and fulfill. I was able to identify the major broken areas of my life in order to move forward into my PURPOSE.

1.) A father's rejection, absence, and abandonment can be more damaging than the eyes can see. I longed for my father's attention, his love, his nurturing, his safety, and his protection. I could not understand why this man left me. Yet he continued to raise his other set of children in the same town. This left me wounded and reckless. It destroyed my confidence and my self-esteem. I needed my father to comfort me. I needed him to listen to what I was going through. I needed him to tell me who I was. Yet, all I got was silence. The pain of my father's absence and neglect became unbearable. But there was a man who sits high and looks low that recognized my brokenness and He chose to heal my wound. His name was Jesus.

I remember as a young girl sitting in a corner of a room one night, contemplating suicide. I heard a voice call unto me - "Daughter." I was scared because I didn't see anyone. Again, I heard a voice even louder saying, "DAUGHTER!!" And with that powerful voice and proclamation, and at that very moment and hour of agony, I felt Jesus claim and call me as His own. I was isolated and alone, crying out for death; Jesus let me know that I have Him to father me, I have him to love me, I have Him to affirm my identity, I have him to provide for me. It was as if Jesus was saying, "You have me to father you now. You have me to take care of you, love you, cherish you". Jesus let me know that everything I longed for in my natural father, He would be to me and more.

The tears stopped falling, I felt a weight lift, and I knew I wasn't alone. A peace came over me. And he said to her, "Daughter, your faith has made you well; go in peace." (Luke 8:48 ESV). He has the power and authority to restore and heal the daughter and the little girl that resides on the inside of us. He has the power to make us whole where our fathers may have broken or failed us; whether intentionally or unintentionally.

2.) Hidden Hurt-Domestic Violence

My man loved me with his fist, loved me with his killer words; he loved me as his prisoner of war!! Love doesn't leave you bleeding nor does it leave you tattered with bruises. Love doesn't have you looking down the barrel of a gun. Love doesn't leave you disfigured.

Walking around hiding what was going on. Trying to mask the pain of the scars and bruises. Trying to camouflage the black eyes and marks around my neck. Feeling ashamed, hoping no one would find out what was going on. Broken by the man I gave my heart to; broken by someone I loved and with whom I shared my life. What started as a love story quickly had turned into a nightmare!

"Why don't you leave?, "some may ask? Out of fear, shame, financial dependency, and children; I didn't leave. I was stuck in a cycle, it seemed. Dying slowly of the very thing that said it loved me.

What do you do when you are in love with your killer? What do you do when you are sleeping with the enemy? The environment is hostile; every day I am fighting for my freedom; I am fighting to stay alive! How much longer can I keep up this image? I am smiling, yet I am broken on the inside again. I am crying out again, "Lord, how did I get here?"

Because He is my FATHER and he loves me more than I love myself, Jesus stepped right in the middle of the hostile situation repeatedly and reminded me of WHO I AM. He stepped in to confront and He stepped in to protect. He made a way of escape from the hell and torture. I was able to find freedom from abuse, and to begin the journey toward a new life. My PURPOSE was greater than my pain. "He will rescue the poor when they cry to him; he will help the oppressed who have no one to defend them. He feels pity for the weak and the needy, and he will rescue them. He will redeem them from oppression and violence, for their lives are precious to him." –Psalm 72:12-14

No one deserves to be beaten, battered, threatened, or victimized by his or her intimate partner whether dating or married. Abuse can happen to anyone, female or male, young or old, single or married, regardless of race, religion, sexual orientation, gender identity, education level or income level. Abuse does not discriminate.

3.) Burying my son. The death of my son Jaquez Santjuan Turner was the most devastating trauma that I have ever experienced. This was the most unimaginable pain ever. The pain never goes away, there are no words to bring comfort. I was angry with God because I couldn't process why He would allow me to birth such greatness;

yet he would never have a chance to live. I became numb to life and everyone around me. I went into a state of depression and no one knew what I battled on the inside. I had to endure the critics, I had to endure people rejoicing at my loss, I had to endure harsh words spoken to me. I smiled to mask my distraught state of mind. My smile didn't tell you that I was empty, my smile didn't tell you that I was angry and bitter, my smile didn't tell you that I was about to self-destruct. As time progressed, I understood that my numbness served a valuable purpose. It gave my emotions time to catch up with what my mind was telling me. There was no support in place for me to grieve properly; no one to talk to and no one who could identify with my pain. I began to open my heart up to the LORD, and I wailed out to Him in desperation with tears in my eyes. Between the wailing and moaning, I pleaded with God to give me comfort and peace to surpass all understanding. I asked the LORD to give me strength for the hard days ahead.

There was a voice that let me know He could identify with the loss of an innocent child. It was God and He knew the grief of losing a son. His only begotten son Jesus died on a cross for our sins. He was innocent and perfect and his death had PURPOSE. God comforted me in my darkest hour and gave me peace in laying my son to rest. Blessed are those who mourn, for they will be comforted. (Matthew 5:4) Only God can turn your mourning into dancing and turn your despair into joy!!

What I Have Learned: Wisdom From a SHERO

- **Gaining Understanding Through My Pain**- I have a better understanding of God's Word as it relates to the pain and suffering that we experience. Kingdom principles operate in a different realm and God has a plan for our brokenness. We may think or view our brokenness as a sign of failure, defeat, and unworthiness but that's not the way God identifies it. It's all about the perception and whose perception it is. What we perceive as insignificant and minute, God considers more than enough. God sees us in a different manner.

- **God Sees Beyond**- It is true that we all have been broken, but God sees beyond our scars, beyond our flaws, beyond the cosmetics we hide behind. He sees beyond our inadequacies, our insecurities, our failures, our hurts and tears. He sees beauty in our brokenness. He sees beauty in our ashes He sees a masterpiece being created. The world despises broken people and things, but God takes pleasure in using broken things. God demands that we be broken before He can even begin to use us. YOU WERE BROKEN ON PURPOSE AND FOR PURPOSE!!!

- God Creates Greatness- God creates greatness out of nothing. God takes the very element of dust and creates a magnificent piece of artwork. He takes what we have to offer and it's always enough.

- **You were broken on purpose**- You remain standing strong. You did not miss the mark or target and you did not fail. You have been broken on Purpose so that destiny can come forth. God calls forth your destiny in the middle of your brokenness, in the middle of your pain, in the middle of your persecution, and in the middle of your suffering. And when you're redeemed, when you are restored, when restitution comes, you have a story to tell. You have a story that will save someone's life, you have a story that will free others out of captivity, and you have a story that will deliver others out of the hands of the enemy. Your PAIN and BROKEN PIECES called forth PURPOSE. God never wastes pain. I have learned through God's Word to rejoice in our sufferings, knowing that suffering produces endurance, and endurance produces character, and character produces hope, and hope does not put us to shame, because God's love has been poured into our hearts through the Holy Spirit who has been given to us. (Romans 5:3-5 ESV). God allows crushing and breaking experiences that will cause us to look to Him. The breaking is not designed to destroy you, but it is a process used to put you back together; according to Gods plan and his PURPOSE. Many times, God will use the things we love and feel we need such as relationships, vulnerable areas, and finances, to get our attention. We can be crushed through rejection, betrayal, or abuse, leaving us feeling as if our world has fallen apart. God uses these broken areas in our lives to speak truth, to build strength, to build character, to develop humility and to draw us closer to Him.

- **He saw BEAUTY**- Others saw brokenness, but God saw beauty. There is beauty is your brokenness. Others saw flaws and God saw a pearl wrapped in PURPOSE. As for me, He has taken a broken and abused, messed up woman with many issues, and he is healing me; remolding me, and restoring unto me all that was lost and stolen and making me WHOLE in Him. The pressure and weight of your pain created in you a pearl. A pearl must go through darkness, isolation, pressure, cleansing, and refining. It's a necessary process; the process where God begins to work on you and in you. The breaking and the pain had to take place. Your broken pieces and your pain were designed to let others see that you can go from trials to triumph and from pain to purpose.

You were BROKEN ON PURPOSE to create a PEARL OF PURPOSE.

You Have The
Power To
Unleash Your SHERO

Author LaKesha Lakes

LaKesha Lakes is a woman of determination and perseverance. From Muskegon Heights, Michigan, Kesha had to take on the reigns of responsibility at the early age of 20, when she became the mother of her daughter, Mieya. LaKesha attended Baker College, pursuing an Elementary Education degree. She went on to work in the school system for over three years as a pre-kindergarten administrative assistant. During this time, LaKesha became the mother of a second daughter, Jade. While working in education, LaKesha loved being surrounded by children daily. LaKesha has a true heart for kids and loved to see a child's special gifts recognized.

LaKesha didn't stop there, she became an entrepreneur by starting her own children's dress boutique called "Day Dreams." While attempting to move clothing inventory from the fashion districts, New York and Los Angeles, a dear friend told LaKesha that a job in the airlines might be of great benefit to her, both personally and for her business. LaKesha was introduced to the position of flight attendant and was hired for Continental Airlines. She immediately had a passion for traveling, while also accruing products for her boutique with ease.

While LaKesha started her airline career to benefit her business, she went on to enjoy an over 10-year career with Continental/United Airlines. LaKesha relished serving first-time flyers; making their voyage one of ease and enjoyment. LaKesha has traveled to over 22 countries and over 150 major cities outside the US.

LaKesha's airline career came to a sudden end as she faced extraordinary personal and health crises. During this time, God revealed LaKesha's true strength, as well as lessons that she is determined to share with other young mothers. Currently, LaKesha is developing her own organization for young mothers, called Young M.O.M.S. (Motivating Objectives to Manifest Success). LaKesha wants to help young mothers to know that having a baby does not have to stop them from achieving goals and they can be confident and productive citizens.

LaKesha Lakes

Unleashing A Woman Not Defined by Circumstances

Going well, those where the words to explain my life. Everything was "going well." My two girls, my career and my relationship were doing well. We lived in a prestigious community and my finances were good. Everything was "going well" or so it seemed. It was the beginning of 2015 and my family seemed to be cruising through the first quarter of the year. While my husband had been laid off, I was still making enough money to comfortably support our family and we were still moving forward. Maybe I was in denial, maybe I just refused to see what was really going on but we quickly went from being okay to falling apart in the blink of an eye.

Everything changed on April 25th, when my husband moved out and left me to raise two teen-aged daughters on my own. This was a devastating situation, as I was a flight attendant and traveled, leaving our girls often. Now that I think about it, there were signs, plenty of signs. I just decided to ignore them.

For weeks prior to my husband leaving, he had retreated inwardly and wasn't spending any time with me or even communicating. He would come into our home, sleep, change clothes and leave. There was no communication, no interaction; he avoided me like the plaque. While this was unusual, it honestly wasn't a sign that he wanted to leave.

In the past, my husband and I played the "Shut Up and Be Quiet" game often. As he was a functioning alcoholic and currently jobless, he did not appreciate or accept my opinions or criticisms and would lash out. Often, we would go into those modes of silence, completely ignoring each other for days at a time. I always felt isolated and lonely. Being a faithful wife, I never shared what was going on in my marriage. Honestly, I didn't tell my friends and family because I knew that they would question why I was still there. This was my husband's third time packing up and leaving, thus I was used to this emotional rollercoaster, but something was different this time. This time I had enough and was not allowing him back into my life; back into our lives. This time, I wanted the hurt to end.

What a terrible time for this man to force me to face life alone. My oldest daughter, Mieya, was about to graduate from Cary High School and was on her way to Tennessee State University. I had to face the financial pressures of graduation expenses, celebrations alone and moving my child to Tennessee. As a mother, I knew that no matter what was going on in my life, and no matter how hurt I was by my husband abandoning his family, I had to push through and not allow my pressures to become those of my daughters.

Throughout the remainder of the year, I did what most moms do; I made it work. I paid a friend to stay with my daughter, Jade, while I traveled, as a flight attendant. Everything was going okay and we were getting by, until my back gave out. In December, my minor back pain grew too intense to stand and serve through a

5-hour bi-coastal flight. I went to see doctors and the chiropractor ordered 16 weeks of spinal manipulation, in an attempt to control my pain. I submitted the doctor's visits to my supervisor and got verbal approval. Since my treatments were approved, none could imagine my shock, when I was terminated, the day before my tenth anniversary with the company, for calling out sick, after attending my scheduled chiropractic appointment!

After about a week of being in shock, I had gone through all of the phases of grief. I went through every emotion and begged God to reveal WHY this was happening to me. Was it time for me to start another career? Was I supposed to be at home with my daughter? Was 10 years my magic number? I needed answers. I also was not ready to share my misfortune with everyone. I could not bear repeating the story over and over. It was time to create a plan.

I sat down and mapped out my budget for the next few months. I quickly realized how fast I could go through my $10,000 of savings. My monthly bills were $3,200 per month, so I scaled back as much as possible and decided to earn a real estate license. I passed the state and national exams on the first try and was motivated to make some money. I was recruited by a national-known company in less than a week and was pumped! Then I learned that I had to pay over $1000 in start-up fees, memberships, and dues to get started! This was counterintuitive!

A couple of months went by with no luck, so I developed a First-Time Home-Buyers presentation to stand out. I also started to drive with UBER to supplement my savings, since I hadn't seen any income. It took me 6 months to finally get a commission check and it was spent before I got it. Despite my lingering back issues, I took a third job at Toys R Us, worked real estate during the day and drove for Uber on the weekends. I missed most of Jade's volleyball games, trying to make enough money to survive.

At the start of the New Year, my husband and I decided to try to "work things out". We had some great conversations and fun times, when HE felt like it. I applied for a higher-paying position at Coca-Cola vs Toys R Us, but the work was more strenuous. Now, this was a day shift. I figured that I was paying my real estate company much more than I was making, so I counted that a fail and pushed on. I applied to drive for Lyft as well.

While out driving one Sunday morning, I started feeling like I had severe heart burn or indigestion. I couldn't even converse with my passengers. That was not like me, so I knew something was wrong. I turned off my driving apps and went to the pharmacy to get some TUMS. I went home to lay in bed, with my "husband" to sleep it off. I moaned and rocked myself to sleep. He could have cared less about my current condition. A few hours later I fell while trying to make it a few steps from my bed to my bathroom. My daughter heard me and came running. Against my will, she insisted that I go to the hospital. I was afraid to go because I had no medical insurance.

Once we arrived at the hospital, the ER doctor informed me that I had appendicitis and needed an emergency appendectomy. He ordered a pre-op CAT Scan that revealed more bad news. A tumor was consuming over 80% of my right kidney.

When the nurse came in to inform me. I wasn't even shocked. I knew I had cancer all along. My mother rushed from Michigan to be by my side.

When I woke up form the appendectomy, a kidney specialist came in to inform me that he wanted to remove my cancerous kidney. He gave me just two short weeks, from my appendectomy, before undergoing the very invasive nephrectomy. I was grateful because the doctor was so willing to take care of me, even without insurance.

My husband had given me three hugs in six days. I hadn't seen or heard from him hardly at all. My mother developed bronchitis and was admitted to the hospital. Still recovering myself, I frantically called my husband to take me to the hospital to be with my mother. It took him two long hours to return home. He was drunk and belligerent, cursing, and manhandling me. He disappeared from our relationship on that night and never returned.

A few days later, I went in for the scheduled kidney surgery, eager to get the cancer out of my body. While the surgery was a success, I had a slight complication and could not leave the hospital for four days. Once I got home, my mother and daughters took such good care of me. I love them so.

Prematurely, I ignored my pain and started driving for Lyft and Uber again. I rewrote my budget and would not stop until I met my goals. I was determined! I convinced my property manager to allow me to split the rent into weekly payments. While this was a good temporary fix, it didn't last long. My property management changed and my lease ended and I decided to move out, to avoid financial ruin.

I sold and donated almost everything in my apartment; giving me money to stay in a hotel for the next ten days. Unfortunately, that money ran out very quickly.

I am homeless. I drive night and day and sometimes I can afford a hotel room. Both of my daughters are living very well.

Mieya is in college and Jade is living in the home of a dear friend. As for me, I have a minivan, a storage unit, a gym membership, a P.O. Box, an EBT card and my creativity. It is just a matter of time before I will return to my previous career! I walk through these shadows knowing that God is leading me. I share my testimony, hoping that it will encourage someone to look deeply within to discover the strengths and special gifts that they possess to overcome adversity! This is my "JOURNEY" and I welcome it!

What I Have Learned: Wisdom From a SHERO

- **Small setbacks prepare you for what's to come.** −When you can overcome the minor things, you are ready for the serious storms!

- **By budgeting, I learned what my necessities are.** -Don't get so caught up in materialistic things that do not matter.

- **I learned to listen to my body.** −You know when things aren't right with your body. Never delay getting treatment.

- **Know your worth!** When you are in a relationship, pay attention to repetitive behaviors and never make excuses for them. Always remember that you are worth the best and when you are not being treated that way, do not stand for it.

- **Never get stuck!** No matter what you are going through, do not use it as an excuse to stay angry and not move forward. Always use your down time to create plans and strategies to get you to your next level.

THANK YOU FOR SUPPORTING

ERICA PERRY GREEN